IN SEASON

IN SEASON

Culinary

Adventures of a

San Juan

Island Chef

GREG ATKINSON

SASQUATCH BOOKS
SEATTLE

FOR BETSY

Printed in the United States of America.
Distributed in Canada by Raincoast Books Ltd.
01 00 99 98 97   5 4 3 2 1

Cover photograph: Kathryn Kleinman
Cover and interior design: Karen Schober
Interior illustrations: Lydia Hess
Composition: Patrick David Barber Design

Library of Congress Cataloging in Publication Data
Atkinson, Greg. 1959-
In season : culinary adventures of San Juan Island chef / Greg Atkinson.
      p. cm.
   Includes index.
   ISBN 1-57061-119-X
   1. Cookery, American. I. Title.
TX715.A87 1997
641.5973—dc21   97-22011

Sasquatch Books
615 Second Avenue • Seattle, Washington 98104
(206) 467-4300
books@sasquatchbooks.com • http://www.sasquatchbooks.com

Sasquatch Books publishes high-quality adult nonfiction
and children's books related to the Northwest (Alaska to San Francisco).
For more information about our titles, contact us at the above address,
or view our site on the World Wide Web.

CONTENTS

FINDING MYSELF IN THE KITCHEN: AN INTRODUCTION 9
EQUIPPING A COOK 13

spring

fall

summer

winter

recipes

spring

summer

Recipes

fall

winter

ACKNOWLEDGMENTS

In the ten years or so that it has taken me to complete this book, I have become deeply indebted to many. I thank my mother-in-law and sometime-editor, Patty Lucas, whose sharp pencil and shaper mind have saved my manuscript from many superfluous phrases and kept me on track. I thank Anne and Langdon Simons, who sponsored, inspired, and encouraged me.

I thank Patricia DeStaffany, whose keen good taste and comfortable kitchen enabled the series of cooking classes for which I developed most of these recipes. I am grateful to Sharon Kramis, Christina Orchid, Jerry Traunfeld, and all the other guest instructors who appeared at the cooking school and taught me more than they ever taught the students.

I thank Allison Arthur, who gave me the name "In Season," and all the editors at the *Journal of the San Juan Islands,* who bought my weekly column, even when it was hand-written on notebook paper, or faxed on the back of hotel stationery from a small town in France. I am indebted to Ginny Merdes of *Pacific Magazine* because she demanded more from my writing and got it. I thank Gary Luke at Sasquatch because he prompted me to pull it all together in book form, and nurtured a shared vision of how some loosely scattered essays could form a cohesive body of work.

I thank the many hard-working farmers, wildcrafters, fishermen, and purveyors who go out of their way to bring interesting raw ingredients to farmers' markets and to the backdoors of restaurants everywhere.

Mostly, I thank my wife, who said, "You can do it," and made me believe it.

I have always cooked primarily to please people, and so my cooking has always reflected the tastes of the people for whom I have cooked. When I was a child, learning to cook for my own amusement, I made sweets for after-school snacks. I quickly learned that if anything was more gratifying than something good to eat, it was getting praise for providing something good to others. There were a few embarrassing attempts to impress my friends and family with fancy dishes that no one understood—least of all myself—but over time, I developed the realization that the food that pleases people most is simple food.

When I first got to college, the work study director greeted me with, "I'm glad you're here. They really need someone in the cafeteria." So much for any dreams I had harbored about earning my tuition by quietly shuffling around the library. For the next two years, I scraped plates, ran the dishwasher, scrubbed pots, and hosed down garbage cans; occasionally, when I was all caught up, I was allowed to cook a little. Compared to dishwashing, cooking seemed glorious. It was so clean, so creative, and, best of all, it made people happy.

My involvement in school waxed and waned over the five

years that followed, but my devotion to cooking was constant. At any restaurant where I worked—and there were a number of them—I found free food, a warm kitchen in a cold city, and a surrogate family in the crew.

I cooked for comfort, for escape, and to satisfy a creative impulse. I discovered home-canning and preserving and raided blackberry patches and abandoned orchards to gather fruit for my kitchen projects. At school, I studied microbiology and small group dynamics. At home, I grew sourdough starter and made blackberry wine. I ate and drank with small groups of coworkers. When I finally graduated, my girlfriend and soon-to-be fiancée persuaded me to come to San Juan Island, where we could spend "a few months" in her parents' summer home and think about our future.

It was a strange and wonderful time full of long, solitary afternoons and bright mornings. Betsy worked. I traveled by rowboat to and from town and cooked for hours on end. The many hours were necessary since all we could afford were the kinds of foods that require hours of cooking. Good cooking has, I guess, always depended on plenty of money or plenty of time. When cost is not a problem, a breast of chicken or a fine cut of beef can be broiled in minutes to perfection. Dry beans and cheap cuts of meat require more creativity. But while peasant dishes slowly roast or simmer, bread can be baked, and preserves can be made and bottled.

One of those long afternoons alone in the cottage, I put together a mixture of pork sausage and chicken livers with bread crumbs and a splash of port. I lined a cake pan with fresh bread dough, filled it with the pork mixture, and brought the dough up around it. I used scraps of pastry from the apple pie I was making to form roses and leaves to cover the top of the thing. Then I let it bake and tried to rewrite a short story.

The pâté came out of the oven and cooled while I waited for Betsy to come home from the cannery. The bread came out of the oven and cooled. The pie cooled too. I chilled a cheap bottle of wine and washed a head of lettuce. I dug out a tablecloth and a jar of mustard. I opened a jar of homemade pickles. I read a book, and it seemed my love would never come home. I sawed hard madrona logs for the fire, and I waited.

By the time she arrived, with friends from the cannery in tow, I had made a resolution that if I were to be in this place at all, I might as well behave as if I were going to stay.

We had a little party in our cottage that night, and the meal I had prepared for just Betsy and myself proved more than enough for the small crowd. It thrust me unexpectedly into the role of gourmet cook and convinced one of the cannery workers that I should go to work at the new French restaurant in town. The next day, I applied there and was hired.

During the seven years I worked there, I put away the short stories and started writing a weekly column about food for the local paper, the *Journal of the San Juan Islands*. Later, I became the first chef at a new inn on the island, the Friday Harbor House. And so we made our home in Friday Harbor and I found my career in cooking and writing about food.

As a professional chef and someone with the dubious reputation of being a "gourmet cook," I have dabbled in some very formal cooking, but the recipes presented here are not formal at all. The food that inspired and was inspired by the essays that follow is food for family and friends. For me, the dishes and the times and places that they evoke are inextricably woven together, and the recipes, if they were presented alone, would be naked and meaningless.

My dear old mentor, M.F.K. Fisher, once wrote, "When I write of hunger, I am writing of love and the hunger for it, and warmth, and the love of it and the hunger for it . . . and then the warmth and richness and fine reality of hunger satisfied . . . and it is all one."

After hearing some of the essays that have become this book, Fisher wrote to me, "Every word seems written by a pleasant person about pleasant things," and I thought she might be saying that I was dull. Many of her most intriguing stories are about things that are not entirely pleasant. But she added, "I will always be glad that I have heard them," and so I continued to love her, and I continued to write about food. We corresponded for several years until her death, and she helped me realize that writing about food is really just writing about life.

Not so very long ago, I prided myself on the ability to get by with next to nothing in the way of kitchen equipment. I was single then, and it seemed there was nothing I couldn't cook with a skillet and a wooden spoon. In those days, I was as ill-equipped in the kitchen as I was in every other area of my life, but I was too innocent to notice.

My skillet doubled as a baking dish for cornbread and cakes. The wooden spoon stirred and served with equal finesse. There were other basic utensils. I had a flimsy saucepan for boiling noodles, beans, and rice; an extra fork for beating eggs for omelets; and a few canning jars that played the multiple roles of measuring cup, wine glass, and flower vase. A clean, empty wine bottle was kept on hand for use as an impromptu rolling pin.

Sharp knives were my first weakness. When I began working in restaurants with professional chefs, I got involved in a lot of discussion about knives. Although I pretended to know all about these matters, I secretly marveled that vegetables really are easier to cook when you slice them instead of just hacking them to bits with a butter knife.

My first sharp knife came to me by fortuitous circumstance. I rented a lonely bachelor's cabin for a few years near a ski resort in Arizona. The previous tenant had apparently moved out in a hurry. When a box of kitchen equipment went to pieces and left utensils scattered in the snow, he never came back to retrieve them; in the spring, things began to turn up. Most of them were useless to me, but a small, well-honed Old Hickory knife became my trusted kitchen companion. Over the year and a half or so that I lived in that cabin, the Old Hickory was bread knife, vegetable knife, carving knife, and garlic press. Even now, two decades later, its thin brown blade is usually the sharpest one in the house.

Over time, my appreciation of good knives led to an interest in more kitchen equipment. In restaurant kitchens I was surrounded by wire whisks and rubber spatulas, and the urge to grab one of these things whenever the need arose transferred itself to my home kitchen. I never seem to have enough of either of these tools. When I moved out of the lonely bachelor's cabin and into an equally lonely student apartment in Bellingham, I began to gather my first lifelong friends and my first pieces of serious kitchen equipment.

A friend from the restaurant where I worked on Bellingham's south side left a gift-wrapped package on my doorstep one day that included a really sturdy wire whisk with a wooden handle. Like a good friend, a wire whisk is indispensable. It keeps lumps out of sauces as well as out of Cream of Wheat. It also serves to break up the lumps in dry ingredients. I never sift; I whisk. A whisk makes short work of whipping cream and, when one grows used to it, puts electric mixers to shame. A whisk is also good for beating eggs, almost as good as my old forks.

Soon after I accepted the need for rubber spatulas and whisks in my life, I was married, cooking all sorts of things, and a perfect candidate for that other fundamental tool in the professional kitchen: a pair of tongs. Before I was married, it was a point of honor to be able to grab things out of boiling water with rudimentary tools, or—in a pinch—with my bare hands. When I was courting Betsy, struggling with hot noodles was playful and romantic. Now that she is my wife and we are a united team trying to feed two hungry boys, it's all business, and a good pair of tongs can really ease the transition from cooking to eating. But tongs must be the real thing, the professional stainless steel kind, not the silly corn-on-the-cob grabbers that open and close like spastic scissors. Real tongs grab like real fingers, without crisscrossing in the center.

During a recent move, when I had an opportunity to take inventory of the kitchen equipment that has accumulated around me, I was amazed at what a formidable battery it has become. The old cast iron skillet that came from my mother's kitchen has mated with a second cast iron skillet that my wife picked up at a garage sale, and together they have produced a litter of stainless steel sauté pans and frying pans. The collection of bakeware that now fills the need once served by my old cornbread pan is staggering. Most of it came from rummage sales and should probably go back to them. The bakeware that I use more often than any other is a pair of jelly roll pans. Rather like cookie sheets with slightly raised sides, these are the perfect multipurpose pans. I use them as cookie sheets; for baking fish and crab cakes, thin sheet cakes, and pizza; and occasionally as trays to carry glasses and dishes outdoors. The edges keep oil from dripping in the oven and smoking up the house.

These days, knives, whisks, and tongs are only the tip of a

utensil iceberg. The Old Hickory knife and its companions are now supplemented by a French slicing tool on which vegetables can be sliced into perfectly uniform, paper-thin marvels. Known as a mandoline, the slicer is made of stainless steel and spends most of its time leaning against the wall behind the cutting board. When in use, it stands at a jaunty angle on its own fold-up legs. Its adjustable blades will cut waffle cuts, fine julienne slices, or perfect carrot sticks. Mine is the Mercedes of slicers; it came practically free from a bank auction at a defunct restaurant. Less-expensive mandolines work just as well and can be found at all kitchen stores.

We also have a food processor, and many of the recipes in this book might not be here if it weren't for this machine-age cutting tool. I never wanted a food processor, but Betsy's mother persuaded the ladies in her bridge club to pool their funds and buy one for a wedding shower gift. "Just humor them," said Betsy. "And besides, maybe I want a food processor. I can't do all the things you do with knives and whisks."

After reluctantly allowing the thing into my home, I quickly fell in love with it and have found it absolutely essential ever since. Out of deference to people who do not own one, however, I offer alternative techniques whenever a food processor is called for.

The whisks are assisted these days by not one but two old Waring blenders. I couldn't resist the stainless steel Art Deco bases or the prices when they showed up at tag sales. If I ever decide to bite the bullet and buy a stand mixer, I think it will quickly become as essential as the food processor. Still, I have muddled through all these years without one, so I assume readers can get along without one too.

The empty wine bottle long ago gave way to a succession of rolling pins. From a friend came a fancy marble one that broke in half when it fell on the floor. Then came wooden ones, the latest of which is an enormous maple thing roughly the size of a column on the O'Hara mansion in *Gone with the Wind*.

The lone saucepan disappeared some time ago, but it has been more than adequately replaced. The first year we were married, we received a starter set of Revere Ware; more recently, we came into a small set of French stainless steel pans when a local restaurant went under. There are oval casseroles, enameled iron kettles, and a really nice *fait tout* or "do everything" pot from France that doubles as sauté pan and saucepan. I use it every day.

As for those innocent canning jars, they bred like rabbits. I have an entire pantry now full of jars that are filled, and dozens of empties waiting in the wings. The jars no longer have to double as drinking glasses, measuring cups, or vases because we now have cabinets full of those things.

I am Luddite enough to see no real need for a microwave, and if you own one you probably know more about how to use it than I do. I have heard that it is very useful for certain routine tasks. I admit, for instance, that the microwave offers the simplest and safest way to melt chocolate without damaging it. Still, I persist in my own silly but comfortable system of melting chocolate in a stainless steel bowl balanced on top of a saucepan half-filled with barely simmering water. When I offer such cumbersome and labor-intensive ways of doing things that you routinely accomplish in the microwave, ignore my advice and follow your instincts.

You might also want to follow your instincts regarding salad spinners, garlic presses, and other pieces of useful but not essen-

tial equipment. As a general rule, you will do well to avoid anything that must be purchased by calling a number on a television
screen. But if you find yourself saying more than two or three
times a year, "Gosh, I wish I had a whatever," then by all means
try to get ahold of a whatever. (Our salad spinner became a kid's
toy some years ago, and I now pile salad greens into a plastic mesh
bag that some shellfish came in, and I spin them in the backyard
to get the water off.)

To prepare the recipes in this book, cabinets full of equipment
are not essential. A cook needs only a modicum of basic kitchen
tools. A few folks out there may have state-of-the-art kitchens with
better equipment than a three-star Michelin-rated restaurant, but
many make do with little more than the single skillet and wooden
spoon that I had when I was a lonely bachelor.

A BATTERY OF KITCHEN TOOLS

THE BARE ESSENTIALS:

*Chef's knife with an 8-
or 10-inch blade*

Paring knife

Sturdy pair of scissors

Wire whisk

*A pair of stainless steel
tongs*

A couple of rubber spatulas

Metal spatula

Large cutting board

*Large (12-inch) sauté pan
or skillet*

*Small (9-inch) sauté pan
or skillet*

Two saucepans

*Heavy 4- or 6-quart soup
kettle*

*Lightweight stainless steel
stockpot for shellfish
and noodles*

A 9-by-13-inch baking
  pan that can double as
  a roasting pan
Two 10½-by-15½-by-
  1-inch jelly roll pans
A 12-cup muffin tin
At least two mixing bowls
  in graduated sizes
Set of graduated stainless
  steel measuring cups for
  dry ingredients

A 2-cup glass measuring
  cup with a spout for
  liquids
Set of sturdy stainless steel
  measuring spoons
Rolling pin
Cheese grater
Blender
Strainer

SOME NICE EXTRAS:

Oyster knife
Sharpening stone
Citrus zester
Mandoline or vegetable
  slicer
An extra cutting board for
  things that should not
  smell like onions
Two 10-inch pie pans,
  preferably tempered
  glass
Two loaf pans
A supply of baker's
  parchment

A 6-cup oval ceramic
  baking dish
Candy thermometer for
  jelly, jam, and candy-
  making
Quick-read thermometer
  for testing the doneness
  of meats
Salad spinner
Food processor
Some extra mixing bowls
A couple more rubber
  spatulas
Pair canning tongs

spring

*F*or several years, my desk was surrounded by large windows on the second floor of a small house on top of a hill on San Juan Island, between the coasts of Washington and British Columbia. The window overlooked tiny Brown Island, a residential island with no cars where my wife and I spent our first year in the San Juans. I could also see most of the port of Friday Harbor, and a long section of San Juan Channel, which flows between San Juan and the other islands of our little archipelago. Beyond the channel, I could see Mount Baker, an active volcano in the Cascade Range, looming above the islands.

Looking out, as I so often did, I was forever reminded of where I was. My view was spectacular but hardly unique. All over the San Juan Islands, equally impressive views abound. One can travel to or from the islands only by ferryboat or light aircraft, and either method affords stunning images of mountains, islands, trees, and sky, dotted with bald eagles, seals, and the occasional whale. Drive down any road and the scenery will take your breath away.

As I sat writing recipes or essays to accompany them, the view from my window changed radically from day to day and from season to season, and so I turned, or rather lifted, my eyes to the window regularly. Sometimes the view was so fine and so full of depth that I found myself drawn into it. Out went my thoughts, like so many seagulls, weaving between the islands, dipping here into a small bay, gliding there across the straits, recalling places I had been and imagining places I had not.

On some days, my thoughts wandered more readily than on others, and it was not, as one might expect, the bright days that distracted me most. It was the chilly, cloudy days, or the foggy ones when part of the view was veiled, days when the mass of Mount Constitution on nearby Orcas Island was completely invisible. The clouds themselves were mysterious territories where anything might appear. Some days Orcas was so vibrant that I could almost make out individual trees, and some nights I could see the headlights of cars moving around the curves that lead to the summit of its central mountain.

Ferries on their way from the mainland would disappear behind Brown Island on their way into Friday Harbor, and I found it difficult not to watch their forms shrink behind the trees and become manifest again on the other side of the small island in the harbor. Occasionally, a tiny interisland ferry called the *Hiyu* would take the inside route between Brown Island and town, and then I would stare transfixed for several minutes, unable to write at all.

A pileated woodpecker used to perch outside the window, cocking his head to listen for insects inside a dying cedar tree. Years after the tree had been removed, my eyes would drift from time to time to the patch of sky where the tree had once stood, remembering the silhouette of that diligent bird.

Bald eagles sometimes soared through that space just when I

happened to look up. Sometimes they were fishing; other times they were hunting mice; sometimes they seemed to be riding currents of air for the sheer joy of it. Always, their coming and going raised havoc for a flock of crows who suspected the eagles of trying to raid their nests. The crows would scream and dive at the eagles, chasing them from the trees close to the harbor and making it obvious where their precious eggs were hidden.

A family of mice lived somewhere in the bushes below my window, and more than once I stopped working to watch my cat terrorize some poor rodent that had wandered too far from its nest. The mice, I think, were drawn to the birdseed that my wife, Betsy, put out to attract the blossom-colored rosy finches, the tiny striped-headed kinglets, the patchwork chickadees, and the everbusy nuthatches. Mostly, the birds stayed below my line of vision, but a car going by, the dog barking, or the cat making her presence known would send them up in a rush to the higher branches just outside my second-floor window.

Those branches, the sinewy limbs of fine young madronas, cedars, and firs, became resting places for my thoughts. As I calculated how many minutes I had cooked a pancake before turning it, I would focus on those leaves and needles. Was the pan still on medium-high, or did I reduce the heat to medium-low when the pancake grew too dark? I would climb and swing, hanging now by my mind's hands, now by the knees, right side up, upside down, resting on those arboreal seats to contemplate whether or not that generous pinch of salt could be described as an eighth of a teaspoon or simply as a generous pinch.

Such were the hazards of writing from a desk with a view. These days I write in a tiny studio, a converted outbuilding

25

behind my house where there is no view. But even in "the shed," as I call my office, my mind wanders freely over spaces far greater than the one it occupies, and my thoughts hang as easily from the rafters as they did from the trees outside my old office window.

Like putting thoughts on paper, putting food on the table is less a function of where it happens than what it really is. Bad writing comes from bad ideas, and bad meals come from bad food. It doesn't matter if the kitchen is no more than a hot plate in the hall any more than it matters if the desk is only a card table in the corner of the kitchen.

A bright-eyed fish, still stiff from the throes of its death, might, even in a cramped and ill-equipped kitchen, be better than some anonymous fillets of plain white flesh from a blue Styrofoam tray, grilled in a fancy kitchen with all the latest gewgaws. Fruits or vegetables, frozen or canned, and served out of sync with the seasons—green beans in winter or asparagus in the fall—are less appealing on a fine china plate than really perfect summer corn or winter pears served at the moment of their own inherent perfection on a paper towel.

For the first seven years that I lived in Friday Harbor, I cooked at a small café with twelve tables, and there were many days when I hardly knew at four o'clock what I would put on the table at five-thirty. The owner of the restaurant would want to know what was on the menu that night, and I could not say. But he was tolerant, for he knew that predictability and reliability were never any match for spontaneity and a chef's caprice. So I put him off until the last possible moment and beyond.

We printed the menu from the computer every afternoon, and it was not unusual to seat the first customer before the first menu came off the printer.

"Give me more time!" I would say. "I still don't know what I am going to do with the racks of lamb!" They were already French cut and ready to be grilled. Last night they had been served roasted with lavender jelly. Tonight it was cooler and they would be grilled and served with garlic purée. As I determined this, I was filleting a fine big halibut that had just arrived from the docks, and in my mind I was already making the bones into a delicate fish broth, light as Japanese dashi, for one of the seafood specials. But should the broth be based on hard pear cider and the finished seafood stew be Celtic, or should the broth be spiked with dry white wine and the stew be a provençale bourride?

"I'll let you know about the lamb," I promised, "as soon as I have settled on what to do with the halibut." Somehow it always came together. The basics were in place, but accompaniments could come drifting in at any time. The gardener who had told me she had rhubarb might arrive momentarily, and the halibut would be guaranteed a rhubarb butter sauce. Pink scallops might still be delivered to my back door, and I could offer a mixed shellfish steam instead of simply steamed mussels as I had tentatively planned. That fellow with the last harvest of tiny overwintered broccoli could make a surprise visit. (This was after all a Wednesday, when I knew he came to town to do his shopping.) And the mushroom lady may have found the wild morels she promised to hunt this afternoon—they would be so good with the lamb. The last half-gallons of my home-canned winter pears with vanilla beans could be offered if I could find a few extra minutes to make those caramel shapes to garnish them.

Perhaps it all worked because it was the café, and the owner was likely to be ironing his pants in the pantry when he asked for the final additions to the menu. But I suspect it was because it was spring, and because it was the island, and because we were younger then.

I started writing those recipes down because the view from my window was a Fauve painting and life was unfolding faster than it could ever be held in the mind, and I felt an urge to capture some of it on paper. Now I've moved away from the windows that used to surround my desk, but the exhilaration of writing from a perch suspended over the harbor has never left me. As for the café, it closed years ago, but the feelings it engendered never went away. And in the spring especially, whether I am walking in the woods, exploring the remains of the garden after a rough winter, or just eyeing a patch of dandelions sprouting by the garden gate, I have the sense that anything could happen in the kitchen.

A trip to the docks where local seafood is sold prompts the same feelings. Live crabs sidestep gingerly across their holding tank, pink-shelled scallops open and close their shells like butterfly wings, and local spot prawns, available for only a few short months in spring and summer, are sold live and kicking or already cooked in a cauldron right there on the dock.

Even if I don't know what I will do with them, I can't resist buying a few to take home. The tails are splendid, alone, dipped in cocktail sauce, or tossed with hot pasta, olive oil, and garlic. The heads, frightening apparitions really, bear sharp little swords on the front and delicious contents that are too often discarded. I like to save the heads and, following the formula for a classic lobster bisque, transform them into soup.

Where I grew up, we ate big Gulf prawns boiled in beer with

a commercial blend of Cajun spices. When I first came to Washington those spice blends were not available, so I began experimenting with my own combinations of fresh and dried herbs and spices. Even though Cajun spices are now sold locally, I find I like my own creation better, and I now think of it as a Northwest blend. In any case, the formula adapted beautifully to the islands, as so many things do.

BEER BOILED "SPOT PRAWNS"
(serves 4)

2 quarts beer
2 bay leaves
1 teaspoon crushed red chilies
1 teaspoon thyme leaves, or a few stems
    fresh thyme
½ teaspoon whole cloves
½ teaspoon fennel seeds, or the head of a
    blooming fennel plant
2 pounds (about 36) live spot prawns or
    large shrimp
Ice

In a large kettle over high heat, combine beer, bay leaves, crushed red chilies, thyme leaves, cloves, and fennel seeds. Bring the mixture to a full, rolling boil, then drop in the live prawns. Allow liquid to boil again and cook 3 minutes, or until the prawns are uniformly pink. Pour cooked prawns into a colander and cover with ice. Toss to distribute shrimp and ice and serve at once with cocktail sauce.

29

HOMEMADE COCKTAIL SAUCE
(makes about 3 cups)

>*1 cup vinegar*
>*1 tablespoon mixed pickling spice*
>*1 cup sugar*
>*1 6-ounce can tomato paste*
>*½ cup freshly grated horseradish*

In a small saucepan over high heat, combine vinegar and mixed pickling spice. Bring to a boil, then remove from heat and allow to stand for 10 minutes. Strain the liquid into a small mixing bowl and stir in remaining ingredients. Transfer to 3 clean half-pint jars, cover and refrigerate. Cocktail sauce keeps almost indefinitely refrigerated.

EASY COCKTAIL SAUCE
(makes about 1 cup)

As good as it is, homemade cocktail sauce is a bother. And though it is worth the effort, there are times when a shortcut is called for. This Easy Cocktail Sauce is the answer.

>*½ cup catsup*
>*¼ cup lemon juice*
>*3 tablespoons prepared horseradish, or to*
>   *taste*

Combine all ingredients and serve with boiled shrimp or raw oysters.

The first real garden I ever tended was in Bellingham. Situated between Mount Baker and Puget Sound, Bellingham is a hodge-podge of streets and buildings that originally formed three thriving towns whose economic bases were fishing, logging, and turning out teachers from the small college that eventually became Western Washington University. Nowadays, it is primarily known as the departing point for the Alaska ferry, and its ramshackle Victorian buildings hold coffeehouses, bookstores, and other businesses catering to the needs of tourists and college students.

Twenty years ago, when I was a student at the university there, I couldn't bear the institutional atmosphere of dormitory life, so I opted for off-campus housing, first in an overpriced apartment on the second floor of a dilapidated house and later in another dilapidated house with some coworkers from the restaurant where I worked as a dinner cook to pay my tuition.

Inevitably, my housing became a distraction from my studies, and I spent at least as much time addressing domestic concerns as I did at school. The garden was a rich and wonderful diversion, and I threw myself into it as one can do only with a first garden.

The plot itself was irresistible. Flanked by an apple tree on one side and a tiny handmade greenhouse on the other, it had been abandoned for a while and was in desperate need of care. It was October when I moved in, so I had all winter to acquaint myself with the plot before any actual planting began. The previous caretaker had built framed, raised beds just wide enough to reach across, and the whole affair was surrounded by a low, shaky fence that kept out dogs, but unfortunately not cats.

That first fall, the garden was full of ruined poppies. Bored perhaps with the discipline of growing vegetables, someone had apparently covered the beds, the pathways between them, and the whole area around with poppy seeds. The wildly fertile soil responded with everything it had, and I was left with a thousand porcelain ginger-jar seedpods that rode their slender stalks through the first few rains and then turned in for winter. I turned the soil two or three times with shovel and pitchfork and read books about gardening. I ordered seeds, browsed through almanacs, and waited for spring.

On one side of the garden, I built a tepee of long slats, at the base of which I planted melons. I was sure that somehow I could coax those melons to sweet maturity. I housed them when they were sprouts in a makeshift greenhouse of clear plastic, watered them every morning with warm water, and watched with mounting excitement as their leaves unfolded and their vines encircled the trellis I had built. The plants bloomed, set fruit, and then went their own bizarre way. Instead of becoming familiar cantaloupes, the fruit that formed on those vines swelled into impossible white orbs as round and luminescent as moons. Their skin never wrinkled, never formed ribs, and never took on any color. In the fall I picked them and looked inside. The flesh was as white as moonlight and the flavor as elusive.

With eggplants, the produce was not as intriguing but the results were, for all practical purposes, the same. I should have paid more attention to those gardening books. When the experts told me that warm-weather crops like melons and eggplants would not do well, I took it as a challenge when I should have taken it as sound advice.

With the plants that were recommended by the books, I had outstanding results. Huge, crisp chard leaves reached toward the clouds; fine, long beans were more crisp and tender than any I had ever known. Tiny perfect beets found their way into some of my first successful attempts at pickling; glorious salads of several lettuces, chicory, and mâche were daily celebrations of that garden's bounty.

But the singular success that made the disappointments of the melons and eggplant fade was the spinach. One evening, when the spinach was at its absolute peak, I stepped into the garden to gather a few leaves for a salad, and was hypnotized. The moon made every plant shine, and the dew, as it settled, dressed the tomato vines in glittering gems. Cabbages folded their leaves in silent slumber, and tiny new lettuces felt the soil with expanding little root systems.

Cats purred around the low fence, hoping for a chance to scratch the fresh soil, and my dog anticipated an evening stroll. I crouched in the garden, drank the moonlight, felt the dew settle around me, and picked my spinach.

Inside, under the kitchen lights, it was spectacular. Full of water and life, the ordinarily thin leaves felt thick as felt. A few drops of good oil and a mere suspicion of cider vinegar brought it to the table. Intended as a palate cleanser after some forgettable

Italian dish I had served to friends, the spinach, with unrehearsed precision, delivered a perfect performance and stole the show. During years when I do not have a proper vegetable garden, I reassure myself by recalling that spinach, and I keep a keen eye out for wild greens.

Greens thrive in the Pacific Northwest. Many of them are so perfectly adapted to our climate that they wander out of our gardens and find their way into the local landscape. Even in the relatively dry and rocky San Juans, dandelions, fennel, and dill line the back roads, wild descendants of herbs that once graced prim English gardens.

On one of our first walks on San Juan Island, Betsy discovered tender parsley and dark, wild celery growing untended on a west-facing slope. She had me close my eyes and identify what it was she was feeding me. Their flavors were so pronounced that I could not have failed. We were near the darkened shell of a building that had housed workers at a lime kiln half a century ago. A barely detectable spring explained the plants' resistance to drought, but it did not account for how these vegetables originally came to grow at this unlikely site.

They may have been the remnants of a long-forgotten vegetable garden, or they may have been volunteers from a trash heap where the long-gone residents of that old building threw scraps of food. In any case, parsley and celery grow wild there now. Not too far away, another spring keeps a patch of nettles thriving throughout the summer. Miner's lettuce and wild cress are quenched by those waters.

Nettles (*Urtica gracilis*) are at their best in early spring. Even when the calendar still says winter, nettles rear their heads.

Eventually they grow into a stinging nuisance, but for a few short weeks they are a gourmet delight. The heat of the stove neutralizes their sting ands brings out an earthy goodness that revives our winter-worn systems. To gather them, wear sturdy gloves.

Miner's lettuce (*Montia perfoliata*), with its fleshy, basal leaves, is recognizable because the stem appears to pierce the leaves. The '49ers of gold rush days cherished its fresh, clean taste as a break from their dried, heavy stores. They ate it raw and cooked it like spinach. This plant was welcomed in Europe, where it is now domesticated as "winter purslane."

Watercress (*Nasturtium officinale*) and related members of the mustard family are found in wet places all over the continent and of course in the produce sections of our local markets. In its raw form, cress has a very pronounced peppery flavor that is toned down by cooking.

Dandelion greens (*Taraxacum officinale*) are better known to gardeners than they are to cooks. But the variety that springs up uninvited on otherwise perfect lawns was originally grown for its medicinal qualities, hence the bitter taste. Common dandelions can be quite good if they are harvested very young, but even better dandelion greens are grown specifically for kitchen use.

Native wild greens and domestic greens gone wild make terrific additions to spring menus, but to many of us, truly wild areas are not accessible, and the wild patches of abandoned turf in our urban areas may be invisibly contaminated with runoff from sprayed lawns and gardens. Happily, "wild" varieties of many greens are organically grown for local markets, and it doesn't take much for one to feel their tonic effects.

If you don't find any unusual greens, substitute curly endive for dandelion greens, and a combination of spinach and parsley for nettles. The following recipes will allow you to feel that you have reaped the wild harvest, even if the greens were gathered under fluorescent lights at your local store.

SPRING GREEN AND POTATO SOUP
(serves 6)

> *1 pound nettles, or a combination of*
> *spinach and parsley*
> *2 tablespoons butter*
> *1 small onion, peeled and thinly sliced*
> *1 medium potato, peeled and diced*
> *1 tablespoon chopped garlic*
> *3 cups chicken broth or water*
> *2 cups milk*
> *2 teaspoons salt, or to taste*
> *½ teaspoon ground black pepper,*
> *or to taste*

Trim nettles or spinach and parsley and soak in a sink full of cold water to loosen any dried-on soil. Before draining, lift leaves from water, leaving soil behind. While leaves stand in a colander, rinse any soil from the sink and refill it. Bathe leaves again, lifting them out as before.

In a soup kettle over medium-high heat, melt butter. Add onion and sauté 5 minutes, or until soft and golden. Add potato, cleaned greens, and garlic, and cook, stirring, 1 minute longer. Add broth or water, milk, salt, and pepper. Cover and allow mixture to come to a boil. Reduce heat to low and simmer 15 minutes, or until potatoes are very tender.

In a blender, purée soup in 2 or 3 small batches. To prevent soup from splashing out, drape a kitchen towel over the closed blender before turning on the motor. Taste for salt and pepper, adding more if desired, and serve hot.

WARM BITTER GREENS WITH BACON AND BALSAMIC VINEGAR
(serves 4 as a first course, or 2 as a main dish)

> *1 large bunch young dandelion greens, or a head of curly endive*
> *½ pound bacon, chilled*
> *⅓ cup olive oil*
> *3 tablespoons balsamic vinegar*
> *Salt and pepper to taste*

Soak greens in a sink full of water for 5 minutes. Before draining, lift greens from water, leaving any soil behind. Spin dry. Transfer to a roomy salad bowl and set aside.

Chop chilled bacon across slices into ¼-inch bits. In a skillet over medium-high heat, cook chopped bacon, stirring until brown and crisped. Holding bacon bits in the pan with a slotted spoon, drain off bacon fat and replace with olive oil. Allow oil to heat for a moment, then stir in vinegar, salt, and pepper, and pour over prepared salad greens. Serve at once.

A woman phoned one day to ask me how she could be sure the mushrooms she had were really morels, and by her description I knew instantly that they were. "If you're really uncertain, go to the library," I suggested, "and find a picture. Morels look like no other mushrooms." Actually, there is a thing called a false morel, but the brainy, convoluted folds of the real thing are unique.

When the phone call came, I had been burning debris left behind by a late winter storm. Several big trees had fallen, and long after they had been cut into firewood, the work of breaking up the smaller limbs and raking the ground remained. I told my neighbor that this activity had become a part of life. It was no longer a chore with a beginning and an end. It just went on forever, and no sooner had we cleaned up after one storm than here came another. She nodded as one nods at those who state the obvious as if it were some kind of discovery. My yard is a mess. Hers is neat as a pin.

My wife, Betsy, was spring-cleaning inside. Closets and bureaus that had become unbearably stuffed were emptied. The clean laundry was stacked around her, and the dirty laundry was a confusion of changing seasons at her feet. I dragged branches to the fire and raked forest floor. She appeared every now and then with a box to be delivered to the Thrift House.

I was growing tired of the branches, tired of the smoke, and tired of the logs, so I came inside for a glass of water and checked Betsy's progress. I considered the prospect of scrubbing the walls and floors when all the excess stuff was out of the way. She checked my progress and contemplated planting annuals when the debris was gone. Our baby, Henry, played with blocks on the kitchen floor. We stood in the doorway. Time stood still.

Then I looked out toward the edge of the woods where ocean spray bushes approached the back door of the house, and there was an apparition. A pale, pine cone–shaped thing rose from the ground and caught my eye.

"Is that a morel?" I asked, knowing full well that it was.

"Where?" asked Betsy, and we were off. "There's another!" she said. "And another!" I pressed Henry into his backpack and we secured the fort. The fire was little more than a pile of coals at this point, and the housekeeping could wait. A mushroom hunt was on.

The forest behind the house extended more or less uninter-rupted into a kind of no-man's-land called Horse Heaven, where island girls of another generation used to take their horses for ex-ercise. There, wide trails meander through old woods, and rocky bluffs are covered with springy moss and tiny wild lilies. We hiked along the trails and into the untouched ground at their sides, bent almost in half, combing the underbrush for fungi.

Henry watched from the backpack that year. The next year he carried the basket. "Let me pick one!" he demanded in his third year, wielding the pocketknife with aplomb. By the time he was four, Henry had a brother. Erich rode for a while in Henry's old backpack; Henry ran ahead. Before long, both boys were running ahead, finding mushrooms on their own.

This, I know, is spring-cleaning at its best. For in the woods, finding mushrooms, my very soul is refreshed and the cobwebs of dreary winter are brushed away. The dewy pink light of a spring evening, so different from the amber glow of autumn or the lingering twilight of summer, seems, when it is upon us, to be the only kind of light that ever was. How could there ever have been a winter? And surely no summer will ever bring an end to this rapturous spring.

But the bouncing heads of my boys ahead of me on the trail remind me that there were other springs. They are older now, and other seasons have come between the springs. The woods where we first found morels are gone, clear-cut, and Horse Heaven is but a shadow of its former self. The places where we pick morels remind me of the places where we pick chanterelles in the fall. Time passes after all.

Even in city markets, morels evoke the timelessness of the forest, the eternal qualities of spring. Their very scent is like the beginning of the world. When they are purchased dried from Europe or more likely from India, their scent is even more powerful than when they are fresh. There is a pleasant smokiness about them that I suspect comes from drying them in a smoky place, but perhaps it is only a concentration of their own inherent aroma.

Morels are best served very simply. Like their subterranean cousins, truffles, they are too precious, too grand to submit to other flavors in more complicated dishes. If you find a little cache of wild morels, or a single perfect specimen, you may wish to sauté your mushroom in butter and call it done. One good friend insists that this is the only way to eat morels, and the secret, she says, is to cook them rather too long in the butter, until they lose all their water, becoming slightly concentrated and somewhat crisp at the edges. She is very persuasive.

I like to eat morels sautéed in this manner with a bowl of homemade buttered noodles. I also find them irresistible floating in a clear amber broth, with or without a puff pastry crown baked on top of the soup bowl. Of course, morels are also wonderful accompaniments to other foods. The morels we find on the island are large, so we cut them crosswise into little disks like wheels with spokes. I slice them because I know then that they are unoccupied by bugs.

Sliced morels can be cooked in the pan juices left after browning a few tiny lamb chops in extra virgin olive oil. For that matter, they can be cooked in the pan juices left after sautéing pork chops or breasts of chicken.

A rather unorthodox way of cooking morels, and one that makes my old friend shudder, is to boil them in wine rather than sautéing them in butter. When the wine has almost boiled away, it is replaced with cream, and a supple sauce develops that intensifies the flavor of broiled fish in a delightful way.

If you do not live near Horse Heaven, or some other woods where you might find morels, ask the produce buyer in your local grocery if the wild mushrooms can be ordered. If not, you can find dried morels in specialty food stores.

When using dried mushrooms, soak them first. Cover ¾ cup dried morels with ¾ cup boiling water and allow them to stand undisturbed for ten minutes. With a slotted spoon, lift the mushrooms out of their soaking liquid. Pour the soaking liquid carefully into dishes in which the mushrooms appear, leaving any grit behind. Mushrooms contain natural mineral salts similar to MSG that enhance the flavor of other foods, so the mushroom soaking liquid is a natural seasoning. The smoky scent of some imported mushrooms carries over to their soaking liquid. This will change the flavor of your dish, but not adversely.

OVEN-BROILED FILLETS OF SALMON WITH MORELS AND CREAM
(serves 4)

1 pound fresh morels, or ¾ cup dried
1 cup white wine
1 cup whipping cream
Salt and pepper to taste
4 salmon fillets (6 to 8 ounces each)
1 tablespoon vegetable oil

If using dried morels, cover with ¾ cup boiling water and let stand for 10 minutes. Lift mushrooms from soaking liquid with a slotted spoon. Reserve soaking liquid for another use.

Slice morels into ¼-inch rings. In a deep saucepan over medium heat, combine morels and wine. Allow wine to boil until it has almost cooked away and mushrooms can be heard starting to sizzle. When wine is almost gone, pour in cream and bring to a boil. Watch closely and stir to prevent boiling over. Boil until cream is slightly thickened and sauce is reduced to about half its original volume. Season to taste with salt and pepper. Keep sauce warm while broiling salmon.

Position rack 6 inches from heating element, and preheat

broiler. Place salmon fillets on a broiler pan and brush with oil. Broil 5 minutes with oven door closed, then turn off oven and bake salmon 5 minutes longer without opening the door. With a metal spatula, transfer broiled fillets to serving plates, pour morel sauce over them, and serve at once.

RISOTTO WITH ASPARAGUS, SAFFRON, AND MORELS
(serves 4)

1 pound fresh morels, or ¾ cup dried
2 tablespoons olive oil
2 tablespoons butter
1 large onion, peeled and finely chopped
3 or 4 cloves garlic, crushed or finely chopped
1 cup Arborio or other short-grain rice
½ cup white wine
3 to 3½ cups chicken or vegetable broth, as needed
½ pound asparagus tips, cut into 1-inch lengths
½ cup freshly grated Parmesan cheese, plus additional for passing

If using dried morels, cover with ¾ cup boiling water and let stand for 10 minutes. Lift mushrooms from soaking liquid with a slotted spoon, and then carefully pour the liquid into another container, leaving any grit behind. Use the soaking liquid as part of the broth.

Slice morels into ¼-inch rings. In a large saucepan over

medium-high heat, sauté mushrooms in olive oil 3 minutes, then transfer to a dish and set aside.

Melt butter in pan in which mushrooms were sautéed, add chopped onion, and sauté over medium heat for 5 minutes, or until soft and beginning to brown. Add garlic and rice and sauté 2 to 3 minutes more, or until rice is coated with butter and heated through. Do not allow garlic to brown.

Pour in white wine and stir until wine is absorbed or evaporated and mixture is almost dry. Stir in ½ cup broth and continue stirring 3 to 5 minutes, or until evaporated or absorbed. Continue adding broth, ½ cup at a time, stirring until rice is cooked through but still slightly chewy. With the last ½ cup of broth, stir in mushrooms and asparagus. Continue stirring until wine is absorbed and asparagus is crisp-tender and heated through. Risotto should be moist but not soupy. Stir in Parmesan cheese. Cheese will melt into any unabsorbed broth and form a creamy sauce. Serve at once.

I thought I was someone who knew about food, but certain areas of my culinary education were unexplored before I met Betsy. I had, for instance, no appreciation for mussels until she opened my eyes.

We were vacationing together on the Oregon coast, camping near a remarkable fissure in the rocks called Devil's Churn. While combing the beaches on one of several long walks, Betsy started gathering mussels.

"What are you going to do with those?" I wanted to know.

"I'm going to steam them for our dinner."

"She's kidding," I told myself, but I offered to carry the little black shells back to camp. I watched with thinly veiled fascination as she bearded them by grasping their hairy tendrils and snapping them off with a flick of the wrist. I wondered if she were wasting the white wine from our cooler when she poured a generous splash of it into the pot we had brought along for boiling water.

While camping, we sometimes carry a jar of garlic, chopped and covered with oil, in our cooler. Some of this went into the pot, along with a sprinkling of pepper and a chunk of butter. Finally she added the mussels. Before I had time to sip from what remained of the wine, she pronounced them done, and we sat down to a small, memorable feast.

I fell in love all over again.

I would never recommend doing what we did. For one thing, our reckless act was probably illegal. I don't think one is allowed to avail oneself of shellfish on park lands. Further, it was unsafe. "Red tide" (paralytic shellfish poisoning) is a very real concern for growers and eaters of shellfish, and precautions should always be taken to ensure that the water is free of toxins before any shellfish are harvested. Mussels, like clams and oysters, feed on the tiny flora of the sea that in turn are nourished by small bits of protein that may or may not be hazardous. We were lucky.

As we settled into more permanent circumstances together, Betsy and I found safer sources for mussels. But mussels should always be as fresh as the ones we enjoyed on that camping trip in Oregon. Never trust the ones on Styrofoam trays wrapped in plastic. You must be able to sniff them unimpeded by plastic wrap. Many reputable Northwest grocers display shellfish on top of a bed of ice and will bag them or wrap them to order. Sometimes the mussels will be open; if they snap shut, this is all right, but if they refuse to close, they are dead and should be discarded. Many people dislike mussels because they have been served ones that should have been discarded.

It's important to eat mussels the same day you purchase them. Before cooking, rub them together vigorously under cold running water to remove any grime that may be attached to their shells. With a sharp knife, a pair of kitchen shears, or a strong pinch and swift flick of the wrist, remove the dangling beards that protrude from the mussel's shells. Once you grasp the beard, the mussel will begin to pull it in, so snap it, snip it, or clip it quickly before the little critter knows what's happening.

Since mussels are delicious in and of themselves, they are most often served very simply steamed. Once steamed, however, they are versatile enough to warrant a little creative effort, and so I offer you the following delights.

MUSSELS STEAMED WITH GARLIC AND HERBS
(serves 2)

> *½ cup white wine*
> *1 tablespoon chopped garlic*
> *1 tablespoon dried oregano, thyme, or basil*
>   *(or a combination)*
> *½ teaspoon ground black pepper*
> *2 tablespoons butter (optional)*
> *1 pound mussels, cleaned and bearded*

In a large saucepan over medium-high heat, combine wine, garlic, herbs, pepper, and butter. Cover and cook until steam escapes. Add bearded mussels. Cover, give pan a shake to coat shellfish with steaming mixture, then cook 5 minutes, or until mussels have popped open. Serve hot with cooking liquid and bread to soak it up.

MUSSEL SOUP
(serves 2)

> *1 pound Mussels Steamed with Garlic and*
>   *Herbs (see previous recipe)*
> *2 tablespoons butter*
> *2 tablespoons flour*
> *1 cup whipping cream*

Drain the steamed mussels and reserve the broth. Allow the mussels to cool slightly so that they can be handled. Remove the mussels from their shells and set them aside.

In a clean saucepan over medium-high heat, melt butter. Add flour and stir until thoroughly combined. Gradually stir in the mussel broth, whisking to keep the mixture smooth. Add the cream in the same way and bring to a boil. Lower heat and add mussels. Stir until mussels are heated through and serve.

MUSSELS WITH PASTA AND TOMATOES
(serves 6)

Although many tomato-based pasta dishes are served with cheese, it would be inappropriate to serve cheese with this one. Mussels and cheese each have their own peculiar flavors and don't sit well together. If something is to be passed for sprinkling, pass additional chopped parsley or basil.

> *3 pounds Mussels Steamed with Garlic and*
> *Herbs (see earlier recipe)*
> *½ teaspoon red pepper flakes*
> *1 can (22 ounces) chopped tomatoes in*
> *tomato purée*
> *¼ cup chopped fresh parsley or basil, plus*
> *additional for sprinkling*
> *1 pound* conchiglie *(large, shell-shaped*
> *pasta), cooked according to package*
> *instructions*

With a slotted spoon, lift steamed mussels from broth and allow to cool. Add red pepper flakes to pan, and boil until mixture is reduced to a few tablespoons. As soon as the contents of the pan begin to sizzle, add canned tomatoes and parsley or basil. Heat until warmed through. Remove cooled mussels from shells and add to sauce. Toss cooked pasta with finished sauce and serve hot.

before the days of video games and fuel shortages and a collective confusion about how to spend time together as families, a drive in the countryside was considered the perfect way to spend a Sunday in spring. Even if there were restless children or brooding teens pouting in the back seat, buds would still unfold their petals predictably, and robins would unfold their wings, and parents could gaze out their windows at baby lambs nuzzling their mothers in the pasture. In the less-developed outer regions of Washington, such options are still available.

Around these parts, drives in the country are regular events. Country roads remind us of why we live in this remote place to begin with. Whatever it is that compels us to drive past, the image of lambs in the fields, even taken in fleetingly from a car window, is almost primal in its simplicity. More than a crocus, more than any tree in bloom, a lamb symbolizes renewal and spring.

The image is made more poignant by the knowledge that those little lambs are more than pretty images or abstract symbols; they are someone's livelihood. They will be raised for wool and enjoyed for their meat. On farms where sheep's milk is used, lambs may be taken from their mothers at a very early age to save the milk for cheese. Less than five months old, that milk-fed lamb is very tender, very expensive, and very hard to find. Lamb between six and ten months (a more typical age for butchering) has been weaned and allowed to graze. The brief pasture feeding gives the meat more flavor, but too much pasture feeding renders the flavor too strong, giving the lamb the character of mutton.

The peculiarly strong flavor of mutton is disagreeable to some, and even the milder taste of young lamb is distinctive, almost gamy, compared to beef or pork. Perhaps this characteristic flavor is why we eat less lamb than we do other meat. Americans eat beef to the tune of 120 pounds per person each year. By contrast, each of us eats only about a pound and a half of lamb. And though more than half the lamb grown in this country is grown in the Far West, Westerners eat even less lamb than their compatriots back East.

The reason for this may not be hard to find. Cattle have come to symbolize the West. During the early years of this century, cattle ranchers, with their burgeoning herds, lobbied to keep cattle in and sheep out, claiming that sheep destroy the grazing land. That belief persists to this day. "Sheep pull the grass out by its roots," states a friend who grew up in cattle country. "A cow just snips the grass off and eats the tips."

In most parts of the Old World, sheep were never displaced by cattle. Domesticated there about 2,500 years before cows, sheep and their young are intrinsic to the cuisines and cultures of the Mediterranean and Near East. Herding sheep is a way of life in the cradle of civilization. No animal linked for so long with mankind could be spared a role in ceremony and sacrifice, and the traditions have followed us from our roots.

In the Judeo-Christian tradition, lamb has achieved a near

sacred place in our diets. In remembrance of Passover, members of many households serve paschal lamb, "roast with fire and unleavened bread; and with bitter herbs they shall eat it."

To early Christians, Christ himself was representative of the paschal lamb, and so, many Catholic families serve lamb at Easter dinner. And the Last Supper was, after all, a Seder, the Passover meal that commemorates the liberation from bondage in Egypt. So a lamb roast of some sort is *the* entrée for a spring feast.

The choicest part of the lamb for roasting is probably the rack. With meat carefully carved from the ribs before roasting, rounds of tenderloin are left attached to the end of each bone, making elegant little handles. This tradition comes from the days before forks, when noblemen and serfs alike ate with their fingers. But perhaps expensive racks of lamb with their carefully trimmed bones should be reserved for more intimate occasions. For a family holiday something larger and more affordable is called for.

If your family is large and your butcher obliging, you might consider both loins with ribs intact to form a "saddle" of lamb. The saddle roughly corresponds to the part of the animal that a saddle would cover. Or perhaps if your family is very large, you might like to serve a "baron" of lamb. So named when Henry VIII bestowed noble rank upon his favorite cut, a baron consists of two legs joined by the connecting loins and constitutes a very large roast indeed. For most family gatherings, a single leg of lamb will suffice.

The roasting method that follows is borrowed from the hills of southern France, where herbs grow wild. There, lambs graze on herbs, so the meat is seasoned from the inside as well as out. Even without the grown-in flavor of the herbs, a fragrant rub and a very

52

hot oven ensure a flavorful, tender roast without a lot of bother. The Garden Herb Blend is derived from herbes de Provence, which can be substituted here if you prefer.

LEG OF LAMB ROASTED WITH HERBS
(serves 8)

> *1 bone-in leg of lamb (6 to 7 pounds)*
> *2 tablespoons chopped garlic*
> *2 tablespoons olive oil*
> *Salt and pepper*
> *3 tablespoons Garden Herb Blend*
> *(recipe follows)*

Preheat oven to 400°F. Place the leg of lamb, fatty side up, on a rack in a roasting pan. Rub with garlic and oil, and sprinkle generously with salt and pepper, then with Garden Herb Blend. Roast 10 minutes, then reduce heat to 350°F and continue roasting for 1½ to 2 hours. If desired, test with a meat thermometer. At 130°F the meat is considered rare. At 150°F, it is well done.

GARDEN HERB BLEND
(makes 1 scant cup)

> *¼ cup whole, dried oregano*
> *¼ cup whole, dried thyme leaves*
> *2 tablespoons dried lavender flowers*
> *2 tablespoons whole, dried fennel seed*
> *2 tablespoons whole, dried rosemary*

Combine oregano, thyme, lavender, fennel, and rosemary. Store in an airtight jar in a cool, dark place. Use the blend to season roasts, chicken, or pizza. It will keep for several months.

53

*I*t is only very recently that I have begun to have positive expectations of salads. Not so long ago, if someone were to say, "I'll bring the salad," I got a little apprehensive. There was simply no way of knowing what would appear. Salad, more than any other body of foodstuffs, can delight, disgust, or go completely unnoticed.

People of my generation have been subjected to so many experimental versions of the dish that we are justified in cringing at the thought. From the fifties through the seventies, terrifying creations like Congealed Lime and Cottage Cheese Salad, Frozen Waldorf, and Jellied Clam Ring were concocted to amuse our mothers and titillate our developing palates. Any of us paying attention to what we ate were horrified enough to look at salads skeptically for the rest of our lives.

At family reunions in Texas, I encountered most of my share of molded salads. Culled from the latest issues of the ladies' magazines, strange, often iridescent sculptures studded with miniature marshmallows were presented to us by our loving mothers, aunts, and grandmothers. The salads were borne to the reunion table with confidence, but they jiggled with some inherent uncertainty, as if somehow aware that they did not belong in this world.

On less-important occasions, iceberg lettuce was broken into chunks and served with wedges of tomato. This constituted if not a flavorful salad, then at least a fresh one. The flavor came from bottled dressing heaped on top. I went through various stages of salad development that included the Thousand Island phase, the Russian phase, the Catalina French phase, the inevitable Ranch phase, and finally the Italian phase. There were occasional lapses into blue cheese.

My generation was not the first to experience bad salads and probably won't be the last. The pity is that we are in danger of losing our appreciation for very simple salads, which can be more nourishing, more pleasing, and more economical than all those wild things we were raised with. The very best kind of salad is made of one or a few well-chosen greens wearing only oil, vinegar, salt, and sometimes pepper.

Plain salads are a part of our heritage as English-speaking people. In fact, some of the first recipes ever dedicated to paper were recipes for salads, and recipe books that have survived from the Middle Ages contain salads that would be familiar today. On a page from a cookbook written during the reign of Richard II, the cook is directed to "Take persel, sawge . . . [and other herbs]. Washe henm clene; pike hem, pluck hem small with thyne honde, and mynge hem wel with raw oile. Lay on vynegar and salt, and serve it forth."

At the risk of sounding like a food snob, I will admit that I almost never use bottled salad dressing anymore. When I buy carefully grown salad greens and vegetables from local farmers or pick a few precious leaves from my own small garden, I don't want to muck them up with something that I may not like or that may overpower the greens.

....

Call me old-fashioned, but I think it's always worth the extra effort to put together a homemade salad dressing. Sometimes this means nothing more than a splash of rice wine vinegar and a drizzle of sesame oil whisked together in the bowl before the greens are tossed in. It might mean something as underhanded as mixing yogurt with seasoned salt and pouring it over lettuce. But a salad dressing that's put together spontaneously to match the greens of the moment is always better than something bottled at a factory, to match God only knows what.

The simplest dressing is built directly onto a salad and is composed of three parts olive oil and one part vinegar or lemon juice. Clean, dry salad greens are piled into the bowl. The oil goes on first. For eight to ten ounces of greens, to serve four, about six tablespoons, or a third of a cup, of oil is required. Pour it on and then, with clean hands, turn the greens to coat them in oil. Splash on vinegar or lemon juice, about two tablespoons for the hypothetical salad described here, and toss again, but not too much. Finally, sprinkle on kosher salt, and pass the pepper grinder with every serving.

My old standby is a balsamic vinaigrette. With good olive oil, there is no better way to dress simple greens for a salad that is to be served before, during, or after a meal. The addition of dried currants and toasted pine nuts to a salad dressed with balsamic vinaigrette accents the sweet and bitter elements of this classic condiment. For more substantial salads, ones that feature special ingredients or stand on their own as a luncheon dish, I like other dressings.

Sweet onions, like Walla Walla Sweets, Maui onions, or Georgia's Vidalia onions, are so good in salads that a dressing may be

built amicably around them. Start with a sturdy lettuce like romaine, generously endowed with chunks of smoked salmon or
even canned tuna fish. Wedges of tart apples and dark green leaves
of watercress are other fine foils for a sweet onion dressing.

Mustard vinaigrette is a reliable companion for vegetables
other than lettuce. Broccoli, beets, and summer squash come to
life under this smooth blanket of mustard and vinegar in oil. It
also makes a perfect dip for cooked and cooled artichokes.

As a final note, I should also confess my weakness for that
old-fashioned oddity known as green goddess dressing. Named, I
am told, for the title role in a once-popular play, a real green goddess is made with anchovies and fresh green herbs from the garden. It is a fine and noble thing. With slices of hard-boiled egg
and big, homemade croutons, simple greens bathed in this con-
coction become a meal. At least once every spring, when the
farmer's market is packed with fresh herbs and salad greens, Betsy
and I choose all the things we need and put together a green goddess salad for lunch. The bright green flavor sustains us not only
for that meal but also through the dark days of winter when we
remember it.

BALSAMIC VINAIGRETTE
(makes about 1⅓ cups)

> ⅓ cup balsamic vinegar
> 1 tablespoon finely chopped fresh garlic
> ½ teaspoon each salt and pepper
> 1 cup extra virgin olive oil

In a small bowl, whisk together vinegar, garlic, salt, and pepper. Add oil in a thin stream, whisking all the while. Use 1½ to 2

tablespoons vinaigrette for each serving of mixed green salad. Dressing keeps, refrigerated, for at least 3 weeks.

SWEET ONION AND POPPY SEED VINAIGRETTE
(makes about 1½ cups)

> *1 Walla Walla Sweet onion (or another*
> *sweet onion, such as Vidalia)*
> *½ cup apple cider vinegar*
> *½ cup vegetable oil*
> *1 teaspoon salt*
> *1 teaspoon ground black pepper*
> *1 tablespoon poppy seeds*

Cut onion in half lengthwise and peel the two halves. Chop one half roughly and put it in the workbowl of a food processor or in a blender. Add vinegar and process or blend until smooth. With the motor running, add vegetable oil in a thin stream to create a smooth emulsion. Add salt, pepper, and poppy seeds. Thinly slice the second half of the onion and stir—don't blend or process—into the dressing. Dressing keeps, refrigerated, for up to 1 week.

DIJON MUSTARD VINAIGRETTE
(makes 1½ cups)

> *¼ cup smooth Dijon mustard*
> *¼ cup red wine vinegar*
> *1 cup vegetable oil*

In the workbowl of a food processor or an electric mixer, combine mustard and vinegar. (In a blender this dressing gets too thick and won't blend properly.) With the motor running, add vegetable oil in a very thin stream, pausing from time to time to allow oil to become thoroughly incorporated. Dressing keeps, refrigerated, for several weeks.

GREEN GODDESS DRESSING
(makes about 2 cups)

> 1 tin (2 ounces) anchovies in oil
> 1 cup green leafy herbs (parsley, sorrel, dill, and tarragon)
> ¼ cup rice vinegar
> ¼ cup fresh lemon juice
> 1 tablespoon chopped fresh garlic
> ½ teaspoon ground blackpepper
> ½ teaspoon salt
> 2 eggs
> 1½ cups olive oil

In the workbowl of a food processor or an electric blender, combine anchovies, herbs, vinegar, lemon juice, garlic, pepper, salt, and eggs. With motor running, add olive oil in a thin stream, pausing from time to time to allow oil to become thoroughly incorporated. As dressing becomes thicker, oil can be added more quickly. Dressing keeps, refrigerated, for several weeks.

59

Rummaging through some of my old school papers that turned up when my mother cleaned her attic, I found a mimeographed handout from a middle school science class. The purple ink on white paper formed six simple line drawings with a brief paragraph of text under each drawing. The text was handwritten, and the handwriting was a simpler, less stylized version of my own. I was twelve or thirteen years old. My seventh grade science teacher had divided his students into small groups and allowed each group to teach the class for one period.

"Teach whatever you like," he encouraged us. "Don't worry about being very scientific."

The little group of which I was a member chose to teach the rest of the class about legendary sea monsters, dispelling the old myths with the coldest scientific reasoning our keen little minds could muster. As a visual aid, we distributed copies of the mimeographed document covered with our own crude renderings of the alleged monsters. Below each illustration we added a sentence-long explanation of how the creatures were fabricated in the minds of sea-weary sailors.

"Probably inspired by a row of jumping dolphins," we said of the sea serpent. We dismissed the mermaid with the same cool reasoning. "A manatee with seaweed hanging over her head." The legend of the Loch Ness monster? "Inspired by the protruding branch of a submerged log." My eye stopped at what looked like a giant, man-eating flounder. "Pure delusion," read the commentary. But the creature looked familiar.

"I know that fish!" I said. "That's a halibut!" Hardly a man-eater, a halibut is nevertheless an intimidating creature. Not only is a halibut a very large fish—typically six feet long and easily in the neighborhood of three hundred pounds—it is also incredibly ugly.

A young halibut starts out as a regular swimmer, dorsal fin up, vertical tail behind, but a mature fish spends its days lying on its side on the bottom of the ocean. As it develops, it spends more and more time swimming sideways, and its face gradually migrates onto the side of its head that faces the surface of the water. The mouth takes a peculiar twist, and the eye that moves up from the underside never seems to fully arrive.

Fortunately, a halibut's ugliness is limited to the region of the face, and most people never see it. The rest of the fish is a pleasant, if peculiar, two-tone spectacle. The underside of the fish is pearly white. The upper side, adapted to vanish into the blotchy ocean floor, is dark gray with circular patterns of lighter gray and black.

Exerting as little energy as possible, the halibut lays low, gobbling up any unwary fish that come close enough to its odd mouth. Some fishermen claim that halibut club smaller fish with mighty slaps from their tails. Certainly those tails are powerful enough, and fishermen harvesting them from the sea are hard-pressed to keep the halibut from bruising their tails as they slap them against the deck.

When my oldest boy, Henry, was still too young to care,

I tried hard to create wonderful memories for him. I took him everywhere and pointed out all the things I thought he should notice. Naturally, he was busy creating memories of his own, and his inclination was to pay little heed to the things I thought he should see. On a tour of one of the islands' finest vegetable gardens, he became more interested in a cat chasing a mouse than he was in the budding brussels sprouts. Harvesting oysters, he showed less interest in the shellfish than he did in the curious patterns made by a broken oar on the surface of the still water.

Occasionally, though, our attention would merge on items of true significance. One such item came into view on a bright spring afternoon when the first halibut fishermen of the year pulled into the harbor. We were there to meet them, and we watched, transfixed, as a giant fish was lifted from the boat's icy hold. An enormous hook was attached to the tail of the fish, and the hook was attached to a chain. The chain was wrapped around a spool, and as the spool was cranked, the fish rose high above the boat and up to the dock, where we waited to receive it.

The sideways bottom-dwelling fish became magnificent in death, and as the fish was hoisted into the air, I realized that my own face could not have expressed any less wonder than my son's. I studied his face, delighted with the awe I read in his eyes, and he turned to look at me, as if to see if I were as amazed as he was.

Even without its head and viscera, the fish weighed over a hundred and eighty pounds and filled the garbage bag–lined car trunk into which it was lowered. Henry climbed onto the rear bumper to see it. Later, we fashioned ponchos for ourselves out of more garbage bags, and he helped me carry the fish from the car to the walk-in cooler of the restaurant up the street where I was working.

That evening, he joined the kitchen crew for dinner and took some pride in knowing that he had been a part of transforming the great fish into a smooth and sumptuous stew.

If you are ever fortunate enough to get your hands on a whole halibut, be sure to save the carcass for broth. Halibut makes a mild and pleasant-tasting broth that can be used for all sorts of seafood dishes. The broth can be frozen and used later in fish soup. Thickened with the blend of flour and butter known as a roux, halibut stew with spring vegetables is a wonderful old-fashioned creamy fish soup. A very similar dish can be made with more sizable pieces of halibut. If you buy fillets of halibut and have no access to a carcass for broth, use a dehydrated fish bouillon or court bouillon, but be very careful with the addition of salt.

Halibut is as easily baked as it is poached. In the third recipe that follows, it is baked and served with a sauce made from rhubarb. Here, the oxalic acid in rhubarb serves much the same purpose as citric acid in lemon, adding just the right note of sourness.

A SIMPLE HALIBUT STEW
WITH SPRING VEGETABLES
(serves 4 as a first course, 2 as a main course)

> *3 tablespoons butter*
> *3 tablespoons flour*
> *3 cups halibut broth*
> *½ cup whipping cream*
> *1½ pounds skinless halibut fillet, cut into*
> *½-inch strips*
> *½ pound snow peas, cut into fine*
> *julienne strips*
> *1 small carrot, cut into fine julienne strips*

65

Salt and pepper to taste
1 tablespoon chopped parsley

In a large saucepan over medium heat, melt butter. Add flour and stir until combined. Whisk in halibut broth and bring mixture to a boil. Add cream, stir until smooth, then add halibut, peas, carrots, and pinches of salt and pepper. Reduce heat to low. Cover and simmer 10 minutes. Adjust seasoning, stir in parsley, and serve hot.

POACHED HALIBUT WITH DILL
(serves 4)

4 skinless halibut fillets (about
8 ounces each)
1½ cups halibut broth
2 tablespoons butter
2 tablespoons flour
¼ teaspoon salt
½ teaspoon ground black pepper
½ cup whipping cream
2 tablespoons chopped fresh dill, or
2 teaspoons dried
Dill blossoms for garnish

In a large skillet over medium heat, arrange halibut fillets in a single layer. Pour in broth, cover skillet, bring to a simmer, and poach gently 10 minutes. Remove from heat.

In a small saucepan, melt butter and whisk in flour, salt, and pepper. Pour in poaching liquid from halibut, then stir in cream and chopped dill. Transfer poached fillets to hot plates. Whisk sauce to keep smooth, then ladle it over poached fillets. Decorate each serving with dill blossoms, if available, and serve hot.

BAKED ALASKAN HALIBUT WITH RHUBARB BUTTER SAUCE
(serves 6)

> *6 halibut fillets (8 ounces each)*
> *3 tablespoons melted butter or oil*
> *Rhubarb Butter Sauce (recipe follows)*

Preheat oven to 450°F. Arrange halibut fillets skin side down on an ungreased baking sheet. Brush with oil or butter. Bake 10 minutes.

With a metal spatula, lift each fillet from baking sheet, leaving the skin behind. Place baked fillets on serving plates and dress each serving with a scant ¼ cup (about 3 tablespoons) of Rhubarb Butter Sauce.

RHUBARB BUTTER SAUCE
(serves 6)

> *2 stalks rhubarb, chopped (about 1½ cups)*
> *½ cup off-dry white wine*
> *1 tablespoon sugar*
> *1 teaspoon crushed garlic*
> *1 teaspoon freshly grated ginger*
> *Pinch salt*
> *Pinch ground black pepper*
> *1 cup cold, unsalted butter, in 1-inch*
> *   chunks*

In a small saucepan, combine rhubarb, wine, sugar, garlic, ginger, salt, and pepper. Over high heat, boil mixture rapidly until rhubarb is very soft and liquid is reduced to about ¼ cup. (Sauce may be prepared ahead up to this point and finished just before serving.) Into the boiling rhubarb mixture whisk the butter, a few pieces at a time.

Serve at once, or transfer to an insulated, thermal carafe. Do not attempt to reheat the sauce or to keep it warm in a double boiler; it will "break." (A broken butter sauce separates into two parts: oily-looking butterfat on top and milky sauce below. If this happens, allow it to stand for 1 minute to separate as completely as it will. Pour off the oily top layer and return the saucepan to a hot burner. Into the base of the sauce, whisk 2 tablespoons of whipping cream or sour cream. Whisk in enough fresh butter to replace the butter that came off the top, and serve the sauce at once.) Serve warm rhubarb sauce with baked halibut or other seafood, or asparagus.

Some experts say that no two children have the same parents. Even if siblings are raised in the same household by the same mother and father, birth order and the changing attitudes of the parents over time constitute a psychological landscape completely different for each child in a given family.

I know my wife and I are more settled with our second child than we were when we had our first. We are older and, if not wiser, at least a little calmer. We live in a different house, and we have different jobs.

Even though we grew up together with the same parents, my brothers and sisters and I all had different childhoods. For one thing, my father served in the navy, and so the family moved a lot. Shortly after I was born, he retired from active duty, and we settled in my mother's hometown. Another factor that kept the family dynamics in flux was the fact that my parents kept having more children. There are six of us in all, and we each changed the dynamics of the family into which we were born.

With five daughters, my wife's family was an ever-changing melting pot too. And there is some evidence that my wife grew up in a different family than her sisters did. We have in our kitchen a bread board that lives by the toaster. It is dear to her because she associates it with her childhood home, where it stood beside her mother's toaster. "I used to butter my morning toast on this bread board," she says. When one of her sisters came to visit, the board evoked a different memory.

"The bread board!" she said. "Oh, this always had Mom's homemade banana bread on it."

"Mom made banana bread?"

"She was younger then," said the older sister.

My wife remembers when her mother used to cook rhubarb. "She just cooked it in a pot with some water and sugar, like applesauce. It was the only way I ever remember eating it." But when one of her sisters came to visit, and rhubarb was springing up in our kitchen garden, the plant conjured a different mother.

"You have rhubarb!" she cried with the same kind of girlish delight some women express when they see ruffled curtains in a baby's room or vintage editions of Nancy Drew on the bookshelf. "Mom always had rhubarb when we were growing up!"

"Did she cook it like applesauce?" I asked my sister-in-law. Having heard about my wife's favorite rhubarb dish, I thought I knew something.

"Like applesauce? No!" she said. "She made pie! Mom hardly ever got excited about food. But she loved rhubarb pie, and gathering rhubarb in the spring was one of her favorite things. In fact, it's the only thing I remember doing with her that had anything to do with cooking."

I wonder sometimes if our boys will each remember their mother and me differently. Already, the older boy reminisces about the good old days before his brother was born. Perhaps they each will remember different dishes made from the same foods.

I will always remember that when my friend Jessica was going into labor she wouldn't let her husband take her off island to the hospital until she finished making my recipe for rhubarb meringue pie.

"I won't feel like making pie after the baby's born," she insisted, "and right now I'm really motivated." When they came home from the hospital, the chilled pie was waiting in the refrigerator. I was told they seriously considered naming the child Rhubarb. Fortunately, they reconsidered.

Known in some areas as pie plant, rhubarb is native to southeastern Russia and found its way slowly west until, in our century, it made it around the world. Introduced to southern Europe around the time of Christ, rhubarb was named "barbarians' rheum" by the Greeks. (Rheum is a Tibetan herb that had been introduced to the Mediterranean region some years earlier. It was used extensively in the treatment of digestive disorders.)

Rhubarb was domesticated in herb gardens all over Europe. It came to America with some of the first European colonists, and by the time it traveled west with the pioneers, its medicinal uses were no longer discussed in polite company. Hence, perhaps, the euphemistic name pie plant.

I can't say just when rhubarb first found its way to the San Juan Islands, but once here, it became well established. I gathered slender, strong stalks of it for years from the abandoned garden of a house that had burned down near my own. Now I have my own little patch of it growing behind the house.

GINGERED RHUBARB MERINGUE TART
(makes one 10-inch tart, to serve 8)

> *Easy Tart Shell (recipe follows)*
> *1 pound rhubarb, cut into 1-inch pieces*
> *1¼ cups sugar*
> *¼ cup crystallized ginger*
> *4 eggs, separated*
> *1 teaspoon lemon juice*
> *⅛ teaspoon salt*

THE FILLING: Preheat oven to 400°F. Prepare tart shell. In a small saucepan over medium heat, cook rhubarb with ¾ cup of the sugar and the crystallized ginger for 5 to 7 minutes, or until just tender. Remove from heat, stir in egg yolks, and pile mixture into partially baked tart shell. Bake 10 minutes.

THE MERINGUE: In a clean, dry glass or stainless steel bowl, whip egg whites with lemon juice and salt until they hold peaks. (A single drop of oil or a tiny smear of egg yolk can make whipping egg whites impossible. A plastic bowl is made of oil and in it, egg whites will never whip. Also, a pinch of salt and a bit of lemon juice, vinegar, or powdered cream of tartar makes whipping easier.)

Gradually add the remaining ½ cup sugar to beaten egg whites and continue whipping until very firm. Pile meringue into a large self-sealing food storage bag. Seal the bag and cut 1 inch off one of the corners, then pipe meringue through the snipped-off corner of the bag onto the rhubarb filling in an attractive pattern. Be sure to cover the filling completely. Bake 6 to 8 minutes, or until meringue is delicately browned. Remove from oven and cool completely before serving.

70

AN EASY TART SHELL
(makes one 10-inch tart shell)

> *1 cup flour*
> *¼ cup sugar*
> *1 teaspoon salt*
> *½ cup butter, cut into 1-inch pieces*
> *1 egg yolk*

Preheat oven to 400°F. In a food processor or mixing bowl, combine flour, sugar, and salt. Add butter and process or work with a fork until mixture resembles crumbs. Add egg yolk and pulse motor on and off or stir with a fork until mixture comes together to form a soft dough.

Transfer dough to a well-floured surface and roll out into a 12-inch circle. Place rolled dough in a 10-inch tart pan and line with foil or baker's parchment, then fill parchment or foil with special pie weights or ordinary dry rice. (The weights or rice will prevent the crust from puffing up and losing its shape while it is baking.) Bake 10 minutes, remove tart shell from oven, then remove parchment or foil with pie weights or rice. Fill partially baked shell with rhubarb mixture and continue with previous recipe. Or return tart shell to oven until browned and use for another type of fruit tart.

SPRING BROWN BETTY
(serves 6)

> *2 pounds rhubarb, washed, trimmed, and*
> *cut into 1-inch pieces*
> *1½ cups sugar*
> *¼ cup water*

*1 pint strawberries, washed, hulled, and
     cut in half*
½ cup butter
2½ cups Cornbread, crumbled (page 172)
*Whipped cream or plain yogurt for
     accompaniment*

Preheat oven to 350°F. In a heavy saucepan over medium heat, cook rhubarb with sugar and water 7 minutes, or until it begins to fall apart. Remove from heat and add strawberries.

In a small sauté pan over medium-high heat, melt butter, cooking until it is slightly browned, then pour over cornbread crumbs and stir with a fork. Spread half the crumb mixture over the bottom of a 6-cup oval ceramic baking dish or a pie plate. Pour rhubarb mixture over crumbs. Top with remaining crumbs, pressing the top layer of crumbs into the rhubarb to moisten. Bake 40 minutes, or until well browned. Serve hot with whipped cream or plain yogurt.

summer

he closer we get to the summer solstice, the closer I come to the edge. The days grow longer and the nights grow shorter. I feel the planet tilting, and I wonder sometimes if I might be sliding off. When I finally collapse into bed every night at eleven to lie awake and stare at the ceiling, the signs of twilight are still written plainly on the southern sky, and when at six or seven o'clock, I finally admit that I am awake and get up, the sun is already high. So I sleep less and less and grow more and more irritable. I catch glimpses of myself in the mirror, and I'm reminded of those old horror movies like *Dr. Jekyll and Mr. Hyde*. Who is that nutcase?

At the same time, I feel strangely elated. I laugh easily and readily. I give ridiculous answers to reasonable questions and respond inappropriately to all sorts of situations.

I grew up in Florida, close to the equator, where the summer solstice isn't much different from the winter solstice and everyone behaves strangely all the time. When my third grade teacher explained that in the north it stayed light longer in summer, I was intrigued. I memorized the words to that old Robert Louis Stevenson poem: "In winter I get up at night / and dress by yellow candle light. / In summer quite the other way, / I have to go to bed by day." But I never expected this information to have any bearing on my life. I guess I didn't really believe her. She was the same woman who told us about fireflies. Since there are no fireflies in Florida, I had never seen those mythical creatures, and while I was willing to accept that they did exist, the information entered only the periphery of my awareness. This was a reality that had little to do with me.

I didn't give the solstice much more thought until I moved north. I remember distinctly the apprehension I felt the first time I noticed that the sun, which had set for several nights running directly behind a particular barn visible from my college dorm window, was suddenly setting in plain view directly south of the barn. "The sun is setting over there now," I said. My roommate nodded, unimpressed. By the time I began to notice the effect of this phenomenon on my behavior, it was too late. I had already established a life in the northern latitudes.

Now, after fifteen or twenty years of this light-induced madness, I realize that it has very little to do with me personally. Everyone else is going through the same thing, too wrapped up in their own bizarre behavior to take any note of mine. This far north, reports of how long a person has slept or not slept are an intrinsic feature of daily conversation, as regular as comments on the weather.

Just about everyone who can manage it goes somewhere closer to the equator for at least a few weeks during the winter. During the summer, the madness is caused by too much light, but no one wants to go somewhere dark.

I have been working on the problem, and I may have found an effective treatment. Brother Peter Reinhart, author of the "Brother Juniper" cookbooks, mentioned a claim that blue cheese is supposed to cool the passions of a hot head, or something to that effect, and so I've decided to beat the summer solstice madness with blue cheese therapy. If this sounds crazy, chalk it up to my solstice syndrome.

In any case, the therapy is delightful and, as far as I know, without side effects. Whenever the opportunity arises, I simply eat blue cheese in any one of its many forms. To test the theory, I had Gorgonzola for lunch in a pasta dish at a local lunch counter, and I felt delightfully calm and relaxed for hours. Just thinking about Oregon blue cheese dip for raw vegetables and potato chips makes me breathe easier, and since the garden is fairly overflowing with lettuce, Roquefort crumbled over salad would be almost mandatory, even without any pharmaceutical potential.

The best blue cheese dishes naturally demand the best blue cheese. While it may not, in the strictest sense, be blue, genuine Roquefort from those mysterious caves in France is one delicious option. Gorgonzola from Italy is another. But even the cheapest supermarket blue is probably just as effective in delivering any "cooling" benefits. The dip that follows will feed six polite people waiting for dinner or two very hungry solstice-crazed adults and their children. The salad, with its attendant open-faced grilled blue cheese sandwiches, will provide relief from solstice madness for hours.

OREGON BLUE CHEESE DIP
(makes about 1½ cups)

> 4 ounces Oregon blue cheese
> ¼ cup mayonnaise
> ¾ cup plain nonfat yogurt

1 tablespoon lemon juice, or to taste
Freshly ground black pepper to taste

In a small bowl, crumble blue cheese with a fork and stir in mayonnaise. Stir in yogurt, lemon juice, and a generous grind of pepper. Grind a little more pepper over the top. Serve with carrot sticks, celery sticks, broccoli spears, radishes, and potato chips.

SALAD WITH GORGONZOLA TOASTS
(serves 4)

1 head green or red leaf lettuce
24 slices French bread (½ inch thick)
4 ounces Gorgonzola cheese
¼ cup butter, melted
⅓ cup olive oil
2 tablespoons lemon juice
Kosher salt to taste
Freshly ground black pepper to taste

Break the lettuce leaves into bite-sized pieces, wash in cold water, and spin dry; set aside.

Preheat broiler. Arrange French bread slices on a baking sheet and toast on one side. In a small bowl, stir together blue cheese and melted butter to make a fairly smooth paste. Spread cheese mixture on the untoasted side of each slice of bread, arrange toasts on a baking sheet, and set aside.

In a large salad bowl, toss prepared lettuce with olive oil, making sure each leaf is coated, then toss briefly with lemon juice. (The oil coating will temporarily protect the leaves from the wilting effects of the lemon juice and salt.) Sprinkle with salt to taste, then divide salad among four plates. Place cheese-covered toasts under broiler for 1 minute, or until bubbling hot, then divide hot cheese toasts among salads. Sprinkle with freshly ground black pepper and serve at once.

*E*very time I close my eyes, I see sunflowers. Behind the sunflowers I see berry vines and vegetables growing in profusion. I drift around in this reverie until I open my eyes and get back to whatever it is I am supposed to be doing.

This goes on for weeks every time I visit White Point Farm, where my friends Kappy and Bob Rautenberg grow huge sunflowers around their extensive berry patch. After clearing away acres of wild rosebushes and digging a small pond to dry out the boggy ground in which the roses grew, the Rautenbergs have developed an irrigation system that could put entire civilizations to shame.

The pond water is ingeniously drawn into a system of hoses and sprinklers that keeps rows of peas, beans, greens, and corn thriving. It also serves, of course, to water the berries, which are the principal crop of the little farm near Roche Harbor on the north end of San Juan Island.

Blueberries, boysenberries, marionberries, raspberries, loganberries, and strawberries thrive under yards of protective netting that keeps out the birds and forms a sort of cathedral ceiling over the vines. Inside the nets, where wasps are trapped in buckets of water baited with salmon, an eerie stillness prevails over the ripening berries.

It is that stillness that haunts me and visits my quiet moments with images of sunflowers. Here in town, ferryboat horns and seaplanes shake the sky every five minutes, cars roll by in a steady stream, and the harbor is bustling with activity all summer long. Stillness is at a premium. On more remote reaches of the island, like White Point Farm, the peace is a tangible thing.

Behind their house, the Rautenbergs have a patio surrounded by a high fence and furnished with raised beds of herbs and flowers. In the center of the patio is a wooden table. The first time I visited them, the table was spread with greens from the garden, cold roast chicken, cold pasta, smoked salmon, crackers, cream cheese, capers, and several kinds of fresh berries piled in china bowls.

A summer lunch like that one is more than something to be enjoyed for a moment or an hour or even a day. It is a piece of time polished to a warm glow, set apart from other times, to be pulled out like a worry stone and revisited whenever the conscious mind stumbles across it. So I am not disturbed by these images of sunflowers; I rather enjoy them, and I'll try to sustain them for a while. One thing that helps is eating berries. I find it impossible now to eat berries from anywhere else without comparing them to Kappy and Bob's.

The strawberries I eat most often are from the man who taught the Rautenbergs how to grow strawberries in the islands. Dr. Hugh Lawrence, a retired heart surgeon, took up growing berries when he settled on an island farm in the eighties. Dr. Lawrence installs new plants every spring. He weeds, waters, and gathers the berries himself, and delivers them to bed and breakfasts and a handful of select restaurants in Friday Harbor.

83

The Rautenbergs deliver their berries only to Roche Harbor, a stone's throw from their home on White Point. Kappy and Lawrence have developed a friendly rivalry. "When we started growing strawberries," admits Kappy, "I called Hugh and asked him what he did, and he told me, and we did it. But," she adds emphatically, holding up a specimen as evidence, "our berries are better!"

Dr. Lawrence, who takes his berries very seriously, disagrees. "Kappy's berries are bigger," he says, in a voice that bears all the authority of his New England heritage, "but they're not as flavorful as mine. Maybe she waters them too much." Lawrence could be joking, but it's hard to say. "A really good strawberry is red and sweet." He holds up an example. "It has no white shoulders, and," at this point he bites the berry and exposes its innards, "it has no white pith. Kappy's berries are all pith." He can't help smiling now.

"Hugh just doesn't water his berries enough," asserts Kappy. "I think if he would just water them, they'd be as big as mine. And of course my water is like a fertilizer." Truly, the Rautenbergs' water is rich in minerals and natural organic material from the algae that grows in their pond. "Now look at this berry," she says.

I admit that it's bigger and shinier, but I will have to keep eating for years before I ever determine whether one farmer's berry is really better than the other's. The only way to tell, or not to tell, as the case may be, is to make batch after batch of perfect shortcake and serve it with copious amounts of strawberries. The strawberries should be perfectly vine ripened and, if possible, never exposed to the rigors of refrigeration. The shortbread should be tender and hot and made with very soft flour. I compensate for the hardness of all-purpose flour by cutting it with cornstarch.

84

When the season is winding down, a few strawberries should be frozen to brighten the dark days that lie between strawberry seasons. The frozen strawberries lose the texture that makes them so wonderful when they are fresh, but their bright color and lively scent is still a welcome addition to winter desserts. Thaw and purée the berries to use as a sauce, or transform them into sorbet.

STRAWBERRY SHORTCAKE
(serves 6)

Perfect Shortcake (recipe follows)
2 tablespoons lemon juice
¼ cup sugar
2 pints red, ripe strawberries,
*   rinsed and drained*
1 cup whipping cream
¼ cup powdered sugar
1 teaspoon vanilla extract
Mint or lemon balm sprigs for garnish

Prepare shortcake. While it bakes, prepare strawberries. In a mixing bowl, combine lemon juice and sugar. With a sharp paring knife, trim green crown from each strawberry, removing as little fruit as possible. Cut the strawberries in half lengthwise and drop them as they are sliced into the mixture of lemon juice and sugar. Toss strawberries lightly in this syrup and allow to stand while cream is whipped.

In a chilled mixing bowl, whip cream with a wire whisk just until it begins to hold soft peaks. Add powdered sugar and vanilla extract, and stir just until they disappear. Do not overwhip, or cream will be grainy. Transfer whipped cream to a self-sealing food

85

storage bag and cut 1 inch off one corner of the bag to form an impromptu pastry bag.

Cut each shortcake in half horizontally, then pile prepared berries onto bottom halves of shortcakes. Pipe a dollop of whipped cream on top of the berries, then replace top layer of shortbread at a jaunty angle. Tuck a sprig of mint or lemon balm at the intersection of berries and shortcake. Serve at once.

PERFECT SHORTCAKE
(makes 6 large biscuits)

> *1 ¾ cups flour*
> *¼ cup cornstarch*
> *2 tablespoons powdered sugar*
> *2 teaspoons baking powder*
> *½ teaspoon salt*
> *¾ cup cold butter, cut into 1-inch pieces*
> *¾ cup milk*

Preheat oven to 400°F. In a food processor or mixing bowl, combine flour, cornstarch, sugar, baking powder, and salt. Add butter and mix with a fork or process, pulsing the motor on and off, until the mixture resembles crumbs. Add milk all at once and stir or process briefly to form a soft dough. Turn dough out onto a well-floured surface and knead very lightly. Do not overwork dough or shortcakes will be tough. Roll dough into a 6-inch square, trim edges, then cut into three long rectangles. Cut each rectangle in half to form 6 neat cakes, each about 2 by 3 inches. Arrange cakes a few inches apart on a baking sheet and bake on top rack of preheated oven for 12 minutes, or until tops are browned.

TO FREEZE STRAWBERRIES
Fresh strawberries

Line a pan that fits easily on a freezer shelf with aluminum foil or baker's parchment. Rinse the strawberries and drain them in a colander. With a sharp paring knife, trim each berry, removing the crown with as little fruit attached as possible. Arranging them so that they do not touch, place the berries one by one, cut side down, on the lined sheet, and freeze for several hours or overnight. When the berries are frozen solid, transfer to self-sealing food storage bags and store at 0°F or colder.

AMAZING STRAWBERRY SORBET
(serves 6)

> *1 pound whole, frozen strawberries*
> *1 cup cold water*
> *1 cup sugar*
> *2 tablespoons balsamic or raspberry vinegar*
> *Mint leaves (optional)*

In a food processor with a grater attachment, grate the frozen strawberries. In a chilled bowl, combine water, sugar, and balsamic or raspberry vinegar. Stir in grated frozen berries and transfer to a freezer storage container to set. Garnish each serving with fresh mint leaves, if desired.

FRESH STRAWBERRY SORBET
(makes about 3 cups)

While Amazing Strawberry Sorbet is wonderful because it utilizes frozen strawberries and can bring a taste of summer in winter, Fresh Strawberry Sorbet is for summer, when perfectly ripe, fresh, local strawberries are coming out of your ears and threatening to spoil faster than you can eat them. It buys you a little time and makes a fantastic dessert.

1 pint red, ripe strawberries,
    hulled and sliced
¾ cup water
¾ cup sugar
2 tablespoons lemon juice
Additional fresh strawberries for garnish

In a mixing bowl, mash strawberries with sugar; continue mashing until the strawberries are practically liquefied. Stir in water and lemon juice, then transfer mixture all at once to an old-fashioned aluminum ice cube tray or a cake pan. (Aluminum is good here because it conducts heat well and allows the sorbet to freeze quickly.)

After 30 minutes, remove the mixture from the freezer and stir with a fork to break up any ice crystals that may have formed. Repeat this process every 30 minutes, until mixture is frozen to desired consistency. Garnish each serving with a few fresh strawberries.

88
....

On August of 1993, *Harper's* magazine published a story by Jonathan Raban about the Pacific Northwest called "The Next Last Frontier." Following highways from Seattle to Missoula and west again to the Olympic Peninsula, Raban explored the region, marking the qualities that distinguish it from other parts of the country. Giant trees, larger-than-life clear-cuts, the stark hills that bank the Columbia River, soaring eagles, and the Space Needle in Seattle decorate his evocative word picture of the Northwest.

The reader is offered a Northwest that is rugged, untamed, and, of course, outdoors. But a closer reading reveals a landscape of interiors. The giant trees and the soaring eagle are viewed from inside an apartment on Seattle's Queen Anne Hill. The Columbia and the clear-cuts are seen from the windows of a car moving along the interstate. The scale of the place and the Space Needle are apparently contemplated while the writer is perched on a barstool somewhere in Montana.

Even for those of us who dwell here, ostensibly enjoying the great outdoor lifestyle, the bulk of our time is consumed by hours spent indoors. Taking in the scenery—actually looking at the raw-edged vistas that constitute the spirit of the place—takes a conscious effort, a willful shift of priorities.

....

One summer morning, after Betsy and I had fortified ourselves and our son, Henry, with blueberries and bacon, we pushed
away the breakfast dishes and reviewed our mental list of things
to do. We were preparing our home for the arrival of our second
child, who was due to arrive any day. For several months prior to
the arrival of the baby, this had been a daily activity. Storage space
had been reorganized. Furniture had been rearranged to accom-
modate the cradle, the new dresser, and the changing table. The
laundry room had been emptied, cleaned, and refilled. The floors
still needed mopping and waxing, and—if we could possibly get
to it—the baby's room still needed painting.

Before we finished our coffee, before we finished the lists of
what had been done and what still needed doing, I was, in my
mind, skipping over giant rocks that tumble into the Strait of
Juan de Fuca off South Beach. I admitted that I had not heard a
word that had been said, and through an almost unspoken agree-
ment, we postponed our household duties, packed up Henry and
the dog, and made our way to the windswept side of the island.
Over the glacier-scraped fields, we half-walked, half-ran. The
grass billowed like waves before us, and the clouds parted in the
sky above us. Crows called, eagles soared, and seedpods rattled in
the breeze like tiny paper maracas along the trail.

We landed, breathless, on the beach. Henry found tide pools
to explore, the dog found sticks to fetch, and Betsy found the
kind of air she had been longing for. Her face lifted to a point
somewhere off the horizon and she drank in the sunlight, the sea
breeze, and that intangible stuff of her native Northwest that fills
her with strength. Her hair contained all the colors of the late
summer grass. Offshore, a salmon leapt from the water and

sparkled before us like a vision.

The salmon jumping was like an exclamation point on the end of a perfect escape from the indoors. But soon, inside my head, I was back indoors cooking the salmon, preparing the fish in a way that might convey to those who ate it all that it stood for.

In Liguria, the region of Italy that abuts the French Riviera, cooks are famous for their light touch with seafood, and it is said that they simply "take fish from the sea and warm it up." Tiny smelts are rolled in flour and fried whole, to be eaten head and all. Squid are sliced into perfect disks and fried the same way. Whole rockfish are baked in brick ovens and brought to the table with a dish of green olive oil and sections of fresh lemons and oranges to be ladled over the fish. But those are different fish in a different place.

To bring wild salmon to the table in a manner befitting its environment, I mused, gazing at the spot where the salmon had jumped, a cook would have to draw on the traditions of the area. One could smoke the fish over a slow alder fire, bake the fillets on a plank of cedar, or, in the modern tradition, oven-broil it with a generous sprinkling of Johnny's seafood seasoning, a commercial blend of salt, spices, and MSG popular with Northwest cooks. But these traditions are too tame, too confining for a fish with origins so noble and wild. Better, I thought that day, to draw on my instincts and create a dish as spontaneous as the leap from the water that inspired it.

A few days later, the family was gathered around a table on the lawn. The new baby, William Erich, had been born, and we called him Erich, after Betsy's father. While he nursed, I grilled salmon fillets over a charcoal fire and whisked a sauce made with fresh raspberries. Since then, I have made that same sauce with wild blackberries and with the claret-colored berries of my neighbor's red currant bush. I have also used salmonberries and thimbleber-ries. The acid edge of fresh berries cuts like a sword through rich fish like salmon, rather the way a wedge of fresh lemon cuts into fish from the Mediterranean Sea.

Demonstrating the recipe for friends one summer, I picked up a technique for grilling lots of salmon at once. Instead of plac-ing the salmon directly on the grill, my friend sandwiches the well-oiled fillets between two wire cooling racks, the kind profes-sional bakers use, and grills up to a dozen individual portions all at once. Wearing heavy oven mitts, he grabs the pair of cooling racks as soon as the fillets are cooked on one side and flips them to grill the other side. When the other side is cooked, the whole affair is lifted from the grill and, with a wide spatula, the individ-ual fillets are transferred to a serving platter or individual plates.

GRILLED SALMON WITH WARM RASPBERRY BUTTER SAUCE
(serves 6)

> *Raspberry Butter Sauce (recipe follows)*
> *1 side of salmon (3 pounds), skinned and cut into six 8-ounce fillets*
> *2 tablespoons vegetable oil*
> *½ pint fresh raspberries for garnish*

Prepare Raspberry Butter Sauce. In a backyard barbecue, build a fire of seasoned hardwood or commercial charcoal. Allow fire to blaze and then settle into hot, white ash.

Warm a large platter or 6 dinner plates in a 250°F oven. Position grill rack 4 to 6 inches above glowing coals and wipe with an oily cloth.

Coat fillets generously with oil. Place fillets, skinned side up, onto rack and grill 5 minutes. If oil ignites, cool flames with a little water, splashed from a cup or streamed from a squirt gun. With a long spatula, turn once and grill 5 minutes more. Transfer fillets from grill to warmed platter or dinner plates and serve with a few raspberries sprinkled around each fillet. Pass warm Raspberry Butter Sauce separately.

RASPBERRY BUTTER SAUCE
(makes about 1½ cups)

> ½ pint raspberries
> ¼ cup raspberry vinegar
> 2 tablespoons sugar
> ¼ cup white wine
> 1 teaspoon crushed garlic
> Pinch salt
> Pinch ground black pepper
> 1 cup cold, unsalted butter

In a blender, purée raspberries with vinegar, sugar, white wine, garlic, salt, and pepper. Strain purée into a small saucepan. Over high heat, rapidly boil purée until it is reduced to ¼ cup. Sauce may be made ahead up to this point and completed while fish is grilling.

Cut cold butter into 1-inch chunks and whisk, a few pieces at a time, into boiling raspberry purée. Serve immediately, or transfer to an insulated thermal carafe and hold for up to an hour.

ɒeavenLy peas

he best way to eat fresh ones," wrote the late M.F.K. Fisher, "is to be alive on the right day, with the men picking and the women shelling, and everybody capering in the sweet early summer weather, and the big pot of water boiling, and the table set with little cool roasted chickens and pitchers of white wine." Perhaps, but I may know an even better way.

On Waldron Island, the most remote of the inhabited San Juans, children pick and shell and eat green peas right in the garden, and there in the flower-scented air, with the sun shining down and the moisture rising up from the well-watered ground, there is no need for the big pot of boiling water, the roasted chickens, or the pitchers of wine. The sweet green peas, fat and ripe in their jackets, are enough.

I stood one summer morning beside the vines at Nootka Rose Farm and gathered peas that I can taste whenever I put my mind to it. Beside me, Linnea Bensel, the gardener, gathered more peas to sprinkle over a potato salad that she had just made with gold-fleshed potatoes from the other side of the same garden. Then the whole picking party made its way across the island to North Beach for a picnic. There, the fresh green peas shone like stars on our plates and burst in a sweet series of supernovas inside our mouths. But Mrs. Fisher never had the good fortune to visit the Bensels' garden, so there was no way she could have known.

Few people make it to Waldron. Waldron is set apart. Separated from the rest of the San Juan Islands by the swift currents of President Channel, Waldron is to the rest of the islands as the islands in general are to the mainland. With no freeways, traffic lights, or shopping malls, the San Juans provide something of a respite from the city. With no electrical service, no running water, and no paved roads, this little island on the fringe of the archipelago is practically a respite from civilization itself.

Culture on Waldron orbits around the post office and a one-room schoolhouse, and the island attracts people for whom this is enough. Those who stay long enough to call it home must know how to make things work, or be capable of doing without.

"Despite what you may have heard about us," I was once told by Don Bucknell, a man who grew up there in the fifties, "we don't breathe fire over here on Waldron." Characterized by an independent pioneer spirit that brought their parents and grandparents to the island to homestead, folks on Waldron may be the quintessential islanders.

"Waldron is what all the islands used to be," says Bucknell. That is to say remote, magical, and above all, rural. The island economy, although influenced by fishing and logging, was traditionally agricultural. The difference between Waldron and the other islands is that, while the other island communities are now driven by tourism, real estate business, and large county government, Waldron is still basically a farming island.

Less affected not only by civilization but also by many of the natural pests that torment gardeners on Lopez, San Juan, and

95

Orcas Islands, farmers on Waldron harvest organically grown flowers, fruits, and vegetables of outstanding quality.

"We have no deer and no raccoons," explains Linnea. "The birds of prey keep rabbits out of the fields." Even the omnipresent slugs of western Washington seem less prolific here. Excellent cultivation practices account for a lot too. Waldron farmers share ideas and collectively practice powerful sustainable gardening practices that ensure healthy plants.

Linnea and her husband, Steve, like other organic gardeners, have always used creative alternatives to chemical pesticides and fertilizers. Protective fabrics cover plants susceptible to egg-laying moths. Flickering foil strips startle birds away from the strawberry patch. Cover crops rebuild the soil between plantings, and garden waste is diligently composted to maintain healthy soil.

During the height of the growing season, flower scents permeated the air around the garden. A cover crop of nitrogen-fixing fava beans planted between patches of marketable vegetables was in full bloom, and the tiny black-and-white flowers were heady with perfume. Giant red poppies and climbing purple clematis surrounded the pump house and seemed to contribute to the flowery scent in the air, even though they are relatively scentless. Canterbury bells, towering blue delphinium, lilies, columbine, sweet William, and sweet peas were also in bloom. Chrysanthemums, dahlias, gladiolus, and snapdragons appeared ready to burst any minute.

"Flowers are more profitable than vegetables, but our market is too unpredictable. We can never be sure they'll sell," Linnea says. So the Bensels concentrate most of their efforts on edible plants. "The vegetables always sell out." In a small greenhouse, flats of vegetables are started from seed. "We just finished building it and we already want another one. We had to build the greenhouse to get the flats of seedlings out of the house."

At Sandy Point, near the site of Linnea's childhood home, the Bensels grow an entire acre of garlic every year, and the harvest is celebrated with an islandwide garlic festival. School-age children help peel the heads for drying and braiding, and adults prepare a garlic feast. Near the garlic field, a rambling herb garden surrounds the modern house built in 1985 that replaced a farmhouse built in 1918.

"The old place was too big and drafty," says Linnea without remorse. The new house, bathed in sunlight and set amid the ancient fruit trees and flowering hedges from the original farmhouse, is home to Linnea's mother, Liz Ann McGraw. McGraw and her late husband, Jack, a conscientious objector during World War II, came to Waldron from Minnesota in 1950.

"In those days," McGraw once told me, "you could afford a little waterfront." A friend of the McGraws, another conscientious objector and a Quaker, had discovered the San Juan Islands while he was in service to the Conservation Corps. His group was assigned to public works projects, including construction of the observation tower at Mount Constitution on Orcas Island. A group of "Friends" bought an old farm, including the Sandy Point house, and divided the property into large plots. The families of those midcentury settlers constitute the core group of today's Waldron residents. Linnea's two daughters attend the one-room schoolhouse that she attended as a girl.

The kids graduate from eighth grade and have to move off island to go to high school and college. Some of them come back.

Linnea is the only one of five sisters who has established herself permanently on Waldron, but all the sisters maintain a foothold here and cherish their island heritage.

"This takes off the field heat," says Linnea as she plunges lettuces into a bath of cold well water, lifts them out, and packs them in recycled waxed produce boxes. The boxes will be packed onto the Bensels' boat and delivered to Friday Harbor. The family makes the trip once a week. A second weekly delivery is handled by a family friend. "I don't know if the girls will want to do this when they grow up, but I want them to have this option."

Lettuce is one of the Bensels' most important crops. Many San Juan Island restaurant menus tout "Waldron Island Salad," and it is almost always made from greens grown by the Bensels. Red oak leaf, two varieties of French crisp-type lettuces, and heads of Bibb, Boston, and romaine are planted weekly to ensure steady harvests. So are more exotic greens like mizuna, tatsoi, and purple radicchio. As soon as the salad greens are picked, they are plunged into the cold well water. The lettuce must be packed for the trip to Friday Harbor because there is no farm stand on Waldron.

With no moorage at the public dock, Waldron has no facilities for visitors, and this, above all else, is what preserves Waldron's unique character. There is in the county's comprehensive plan a hotly debated special section officially designating Waldron as a Limited Development District. In a few carefully phrased sentences, this unique designation prevents businesses on Waldron from relying on visitors coming to the island. This means no bed and breakfasts, no restaurants, and no tourist services.

So every Thursday and Saturday during the growing season, the produce is packed and stacked and delivered to town. Lettuce, carrots, potatoes, flowers, and of course, English peas are shipped across the channel to Friday Harbor. And although they have been cultivated in many different places for at least 7,000 years, only on Waldron do peas seem to have reached their full potential. Peas grown there taste like something grown in the very fields of heaven.

Part of what makes them so good is their freshness. Like corn on the cob, fresh green peas begin a rapid chemical reconstruction the moment they are picked. Almost as quickly as the peas are gathered, delicate sugars in their sap are converted into more stable but less flavorful starches. The Bensels grow varieties in which this unfortunate metabolic process is slowed down, and to ensure that the peas will be sweet, they pick them just before coming to market.

When I make soup with peas from Waldron, people ask me if there is sugar in it. I know there is the natural sugar found in the peas, and I also know that when I carefully caramelize the onion by allowing it to slowly turn soft and golden in butter, I am releasing sugars from the onion, but I don't like to explain this, so I just say no.

Strange as it may seem, I am willing to admit that I often make the soup and the salad that follow with frozen peas. I buy organically grown frozen peas that are actually fresher than most fresh peas sold in stores. Blanched and frozen within a few hours of being harvested, the peas retain more natural sugar and green, fresh flavor than peas that have been picked in one state and hauled to another.

GREEN PEA SOUP WITH MINTED CREAM
(serves 4)

¼ cup butter
1 large onion, peeled and thinly sliced
4 cups fresh shelled green peas, or 2 bags
    (10 ounces each) frozen peas
3 cloves garlic, finely chopped
4 cups chicken broth
Salt and pepper to taste
½ cup whipping cream
3 tablespoons fresh mint, cut into
    fine ribbons

In a deep saucepan over medium-high heat, melt butter and add sliced onion. Cook 10 minutes, stirring, until onion is soft and translucent and beginning to brown. Add peas, garlic, and broth and bring mixture to a boil. Reduce heat to low, cover, and allow to simmer 10 minutes.

Transfer soup to a blender in batches and purée until smooth. Season soup to taste with salt and pepper, and keep warm. In a small mixing bowl, whip cream and stir in fresh mint. Serve soup hot with dollops of minted cream on top.

GREEN PEA SALAD
(serves 4)

2 cups fresh shelled green peas, or 1 bag
    (10 ounces) frozen peas
1 tablespoon apple cider vinegar
1 tablespoon Dijon mustard
1 teaspoon prepared horseradish

1 teaspoon sugar
½ teaspoon salt
⅓ cup vegetable oil
2 hard-boiled eggs, grated
½ cup finely chopped green onion
Bibb lettuce leaves

If the peas are fresh, plunge them into boiling water for 2 minutes and then transfer to a bowl of ice water to halt cooking process. (This will turn peas a brighter green without compromising their fresh green flavor.) If peas are frozen, allow them to thaw (preferably in the refrigerator overnight); they will already have been plunged into boiling water during processing. Keep peas in a chilled bowl while preparing dressing.

In a salad bowl, combine vinegar, mustard, horseradish, sugar, and salt, and stir until sugar is dissolved. With a whisk, stir mixture rapidly while adding oil in a thin stream to make a smooth dressing. Toss peas, hard-boiled eggs, and chopped onion with dressing and serve salad chilled on lettuce leaves.

peaches

When I was a boy, a paneled truck appeared every summer on a certain corner of Twelfth Avenue in Pensacola, Florida. In the back of the truck, small Georgia peaches so heady with flavor that I can find their scent even now were piled in woven willow baskets, attended by a quiet old farmer in overalls.

Since the farmer parked his truck en route between my home and my grandmother's house, we had occasion to pass his truck fairly often, but my mother occasionally made special side trips just to see if he were there. Since he kept no apparent schedule, there was an element of suspense in every trip to his makeshift roadside stand and a certain sense of triumph every time we found him there. His peaches were so ripe that they had to be eaten almost as soon as they were purchased, and so frequent visits were called for.

Maybe because we never saw the orchards that bore the fruit, or maybe because the farmer was shy and never spoke an extraneous word to us, the source of the peaches was a mystery to me. I imagined a wonderful green place, cut through here and there with red clay roads for the paneled truck. There, peaches were perpetually ripening and waiting to be picked.

When we got ahold of enough of them at once, the peaches

were peeled, then spiked with lemon juice and sugar and tucked away in the huge freezer that occupied our laundry room. As long as that freezer held peaches, it was a treasure chest. In the fall and winter, out came the golden slices, as prized as pieces of eight. They were topped with sweet biscuit dough and baked until golden. We ate this treasure happily, basking in the smell of summer that almost, but never quite, slipped away in those mild southern winters.

Only once in my recollection did my mother make jelly. A more domestic friend convinced her that peach jelly was worth the effort, and together the two women spent an afternoon peeling, pitting, and processing. I slipped in and out of the kitchen, drawn in by the aroma and driven away by the hustle and bustle.

The whole kitchen vibrated to the frequency of peach. Pine cabinets glowed with the color of their flesh, and the worn oak armchairs picked up the reflection. Summer sunlight pouring in the window became warm peach juice that flowed from a cotton bag filled with the mashed cooked fruit, hanging from a cabinet door.

In the end, there were dozens of jars full of murky amber jelly, composed almost entirely of sugar and bottled pectin. It would not have won any prizes at a county fair. It neither sparkled nor broke cleanly away from the glass the way the champion preserves always do. But that jelly was the best I have ever tasted. So thoroughly did it capture the essence of ripe peaches that I will never live through a summer without thinking of that day or the days that came later when the jars were popped open to release the scent of peaches.

Since I moved West, all my peaches have come from Washington. I arrived in Washington on a September afternoon

103

when ripe peaches were for sale at the produce stands, and I knew at once that I had come to a place where I could live. They were different from the small, heady peaches of Georgia, but the large, juicy orbs I found here were fine and sweet.

By a happy coincidence, the best peaches in my adult life were delivered to Friday Harbor in much the same way that the peaches of my childhood were delivered to my hometown. On certain Saturdays in August, the sun shone in a mysterious amber-colored way and a paneled truck would park in town. The fruit piled in back was not from Georgia but from Yakima or Wenatchee. Still, something essential about the experience was the same.

One year the truck failed to appear, and I took it upon myself to find a new source for peaches that could match the memories of my youth. With Betsy and the boys, I visited a peach orchard in eastern Washington where more than a dozen varieties were offered for sale at the warehouse. Familiar freestone varieties for canning were what I sought, but I could not resist a case of the soft, white-fleshed Arctic Fire and another of amber-fleshed honey-sweet nectarines.

To save them from the heat, we brought the peaches and nectarines into our air-conditioned hotel room in Yakima, where the boys wheeled them up and down the halls on a luggage cart. Back in the car, on our way home, the fragrance of the peaches and nectarines was hypnotic, and when we paused at a mountain pass to walk among the wildflowers, we lunched on fresh peaches. When at last they came into my kitchen, the canning jars were waiting.

HOME-CANNED PEACHES
WITH VANILLA BEANS

(makes 4 quarts)

> *16 freestone peaches*
> *6 cups water*
> *3½ cups sugar*
> *4 vanilla beans*

In a canning kettle or a large stockpot filled with boiling water, submerge four widemouthed, quart-sized canning jars, and allow jars to simmer while peaches are being prepared.

In a separate kettle over high heat, bring a large amount of water to a full, rolling boil. Fill a sink with ice water. Drop peaches, 3 or 4 at a time, into boiling water; after 1 minute, lift peaches from boiling water with a slotted spoon and transfer at once to sink filled with ice water. Peel peaches by slipping off skins under cold water, then cut each peach in half and remove pit.

In a large saucepan over high heat, combine water and sugar, and bring syrup to a boil. With tongs, remove jars from simmering water. Place 7 or 8 peach halves and one vanilla bean in each sterilized jar. Pour boiling syrup over peaches, leaving ½-inch headspace at the top of each jar. Seal jars according to manufacturer's instructions.

Place sealed jars in canning kettle and, when water is boiling, begin timing. Allow jars to boil 30 minutes, then, using special canning tongs, or ordinary tongs and a kitchen towel, lift jars out of boiling water bath and allow to cool, undisturbed, for several hours or overnight. Check lids to make sure jars have sealed. Canned peaches will keep in a cool, dark place for a year. Store any jars that did not seal in the refrigerator.

PEACH COBBLER
(serves 4 generously)

4 large peaches, pitted and sliced,
  or 1 quart home-canned
  peach halves, sliced
½ cup sugar
3 tablespoons cornstarch
2 tablespoons lemon juice
1 cup flour
¼ cup brown sugar
1 teaspoon baking powder
½ teaspoon salt
6 tablespoons cold butter, cut into 1-inch
  pieces
¼ cup milk
Yogurt, ice cream, or whipped cream
  (optional)

Preheat oven to 400°F. In an oval ceramic baking dish or a glass pie plate, combine peaches with sugar, cornstarch, and lemon juice. In a clean, dry bowl or a food processor, thoroughly combine flour, brown sugar, baking powder, and salt. Add butter and work into flour until mixture resembles crumbs. Add milk all at once, and stir or process just until flour is moistened. Dollop dough over peaches and bake 30 minutes, or until golden brown. Serve hot with yogurt, ice cream, or whipped cream, if desired.

For many years, the crumbling remains of a grand hotel occupied an entire city block in my hometown, Pensacola, Florida. Every time I went home to see my family, a movement was underway to restore the great building to its former glory. Editorials in the local paper, photo displays at the county museum, and creative ideas like transforming the building into a cultural center kept the building alive in people's minds long after it had effectively died.

When the Hotel San Carlos opened in 1907, it was the largest hotel south of New York and east of the Mississippi. Sarah Bernhardt and Harry Houdini, when they performed at the local theater, booked rooms at the San Carlos, and every weekend, the great ballroom and banquet halls were lit with crystal chandeliers and the laughter of happy guests.

In an old home movie taken by my grandfather in the 1930s, the sidewalks around the old hotel are crowded with families watching a parade. Well-dressed citizens wave flags from the hotel balconies and windows as an unidentified dignitary waves from the back seat of an open car. Is it Roosevelt? The last time I saw the San Carlos, the sidewalk in front of the building was covered with plywood awnings to guard pedestrians from falling debris.

Seagulls and pigeons stood on the balconies, and tattered curtains rather than flags waved in the shattered windows.

Even when I was a boy, the old hotel was in decline. Instead of celebrities and well-to-do families on vacation, the guest rooms were occupied by prostitutes, drug addicts, and a few senior citizens on limited incomes, who might have imagined that the hotel retained some of its former glory.

Finally, the building fell into such a state of disrepair that it had to be closed down, but for reasons political and nostalgic, no one dared condemn it for decades.

Sometimes I dream that I have found a way into the abandoned halls of the locked hotel. The great staircase is dimly lit, and I pad through the dining rooms back into the old kitchens. Enameled stoves on square legs are surrounded by utensils dangling from racks on the ceiling. Sometimes I dream that I am not alone. People inhabit the abandoned hotel, as if another world lies waiting behind the boarded windows, where ghosts of the old guests clink their glasses at well-appointed tables. Other times I explore the empty edifice as if it were a tomb where treasures lie undiscovered behind the doors of every room: abandoned furniture, linens, crystal, and china.

My strong feelings for the San Carlos and its power to haunt my dreams derive from the fact that before I was born, my grandfather managed the hotel. To my family, the place has always represented a better time, standing like an island in the wake of a flood of changes that left us scrambling for something familiar to hold on to. No matter where I go, the hotel is never far away, and other hotels and restaurants are rated by their resemblance to that one.

Some of my fascination with the place comes less from its familiarity than from its very mystery. Although we did occasionally visit the restaurant when I was young, I was never allowed to wander upstairs. Only in pictures have I seen the interiors of the rooms. When I was older, old enough to enter the halls without adult supervision, it never occurred to me to explore until it was too late.

I hoped as much as anyone that one of the ambitious civic plans to convert the building into public space would find grassroots support and take hold, or that some investor with vision would come along and restore the place. Unfortunately no one ever did, and one year, driving into town on the freeway on a visit home, I looked for the familiar edifice and saw instead one half-demolished wall of the building superimposed against the blank Florida sky.

"She wouldn't go down easy," explained my father. "Halfway through the demolition, they realized that asbestos was flying into the air." So the demolition was left unfinished for months, with the ruined rooms gaping at the sky as if they'd been bombed. I imagined old light fixtures, door frames, switch plate covers, a thousand things I might glean from the ruins, but there was no way to get at them. The demolition site was off-limits.

The only treasure I have from the old San Carlos is a bundle of recipes that my grandfather collected from the chef and passed on to my uncle. Members of my family maintain that my grandfather, renowned for his culinary skills, developed all the recipes for the hotel himself. Certainly, during his tenure there, he had a hand in them.

"Your grandfather," writes my uncle, "developed this recipe

for rémoulade with the chef at the old San Carlos." Served with shrimp at the hotel decades ago, the sauce is a variation on a classic French sauce, which it only slightly resembles. Rémoulade took on a life of its own on the Creole Gulf Coast, and between Baton Rouge and Jacksonville it was interpreted in all sorts of ways.

At its worst, rémoulade is presented as a lurid, pink sauce that resembles Thousand Island dressing. My grandfather's rémoulade was not pink. It was delightfully subtle, with as much character and charm as the old Hotel San Carlos, where the sauce was the essential condiment for shrimp. For me, the sauce really came to life when I discovered its affinity for Washington's Dungeness crab. In the spirit of my grandfather's piquant sauce, I developed a rémoulade of my own, and in my compulsion to make everything from scratch, I based the sauce on a formula for homemade mayonnaise.

Since raw egg yolks are the source of many fears these days, I coddle the egg in boiling water for a few minutes before I make the sauce. This process effectively pasteurizes it. I then mix the coddled egg yolk thoroughly with the vinegar before I add the remaining ingredients. Making this sauce from raw ingredients is easier than one might think, but if a food processor is not available, or if it all sounds like too much fuss and bother, skip it and make my grandfather's version using store-bought mayonnaise. It is not as much fun, but the results are almost as good.

Once you have made either version of rémoulade, you will be prepared to make the ultimate crab cakes. The sauce is both an integral part of the cakes and a condiment to be served with them. Crab cakes may be presented on a bed of mixed greens as a first course, in which case it is good to serve one per person.

If they are to be the main event, serve two per person with potatoes and a green vegetable.

DUNGENESS CRAB CAKES WITH RÉMOULADE
(makes 6 to 8 cakes)

> *¼ cup rémoulade (recipes follow)*
> *¼ cup chopped onion*
> *¼ cup chopped celery*
> *1 egg white*
> *1 cup fresh bread crumbs*
> *1 pound fresh crabmeat*
> *Salt and pepper to taste*

Prepare rémoulade. Preheat oven to 425°F and butter a jelly roll pan. In a food processor or on a cutting board, finely chop onion and celery. With the motor running, or in a bowl, add egg white and bread crumbs to onion and celery, and process or stir until well combined. Stir in rémoulade and crabmeat. Shape into 6 or 8 cakes and bake on buttered pan for 12 minutes.

MY RÉMOULADE
(makes 1½ cups)

> *1 egg*
> *1 tablespoon white wine vinegar*
> *¼ cup chopped onion*
> *¼ cup chopped celery*
> *½ teaspoon chopped garlic*
> *1 tablespoon stone-ground mustard*
> *1 teaspoon prepared horseradish*

2 teaspoons sugar

1 teaspoon hot pepper sauce (such as Tabasco)

½ teaspoon salt

½ teaspoons ground black pepper

⅛ teaspoon ground allspice

1 cup vegetable oil

In a small bowl or coffee mug, cover whole egg with boiling water and allow to stand 2 minutes. Crack egg and discard white, saving the yolk. In small bowl, whisk together coddled egg yolk and vinegar; set aside. In a food processor, combine onion, celery, garlic, mustard, horseradish, sugar, hot pepper sauce, salt, pepper, and allspice; process until smooth. Add egg yolk mixture and process again until smooth. With the motor running, add a teaspoon of oil and, when oil is well incorporated, add another spoonful. Add remaining oil in a very thin stream, allowing oil to become gradually and thoroughly combined with other ingredients to create a heavy sauce. Transfer to a clean jar and refrigerate for up to 2 weeks. Serve with crab, shrimp, or other seafood.

MY GRANDFATHER'S RÉMOULADE
(makes about 2 cups)

1½ cups mayonnaise

¼ cup stone-ground mustard

¼ stalk celery, finely chopped

3 green onions, "ground"*

¼ cup onion, "ground"*

½ teaspoon minced garlic

1 tablespoon prepared horseradish

½ teaspoon freshly ground black pepper
½ teaspoon sugar
Tiny shake ground nutmeg
Tiny shake ground cloves
Tiny shake cinnamon
Hot pepper sauce (such as Tabasco) to taste

*"Ground" is the wording my grandfather
used in his recipe.

In a small mixing bowl, combine all ingredients with a wire whisk. Serve with raw vegetables as a dip, or with chilled seafood such as shrimp or crab. Sauce keeps, covered and refrigerated, for up to 2 weeks.

DRAGONFLY CORN

For a number of years, islanders in the know used to line up outside a building supply store on Spring Street, waiting for a truck to pull up in front. From the bed of the truck, and from a trailer attached to the back of it, the Rogers family used to sell homegrown vegetables and flowers. This was in the eighties, still the dark ages for island-grown produce markets, before the farmers on Waldron started bringing peas and other produce from their island to ours, before a Saturday farmers' market became established, and before the grocery stores started carrying several varieties of island-grown produce. In those days, unless you had a garden or were very nice to someone who did, you simply couldn't get really fresh produce on the island.

Over a period of a decade, Robert and Louisa Rogers gradually carved a six-acre vegetable garden from a stand of alder on the north end of the island. They called their garden Dragonfly Farms, but most of the eager customers who waited in front of Pope's Building Supply on Spring Street every Saturday afternoon for them to arrive with their produce called them the corn people.

Dragonfly Farms sold more than corn. Robert and Louisa grew summer squash, fresh herbs, lettuce, tomatoes, green beans, and unusual greens like tricolored amaranth and French sorrel.

But it was the corn that made people stand in line.

"We had no intentions of becoming professional farmers," Louisa once confided. "We bought the land to build our home." For the homesite, they selected a knoll a few hundred yards back from the road. Their driveway ran along several acres of young alder trees. Dressed in bright green leaves in summer, the white-barked alders wore yellow in the fall and stood bare against the sky in the winter.

The Rogers family cut a half-acre of the alder for firewood the first season they lived on the property, and when the trees were removed, they couldn't help noticing that the soil beneath the trees was rich and black and deep.

"The soil was so good that we started hauling it up the hill to a little vegetable patch we had planted behind the house." The next year, instead of moving topsoil to the garden, they moved the garden to the soil. Runoff water from nearby Mount Young moistened the ground, and a substrata of clay kept that moisture close to the topsoil throughout the growing season. During the driest weeks of summer, when they did irrigate, it was with unfiltered water from the Roche Harbor water table. Like the algae-laden water that fertilizes Kappy's berries at White Point Farm, that water is rich in lime, which sweetened the acid soil of what had so recently been the forest floor.

"The first half-acre we cleared was large enough to grow more vegetables than the family could use," explained Louisa, so they decided to grow extra produce for sale at a stand beside the road. "Since we had no fence, we decided to grow only vegetables that deer wouldn't eat. Old-timers told us that deer wouldn't eat summer squash, so we planted four rows of zucchini, four rows of pattypan, four rows of crookneck. . . ." She sighed. "We had more squash than we could possibly sell. People aren't really all that interested in squash. They asked us, 'Why don't you grow corn?'"

To keep out the deer, Robert and Louisa fashioned a fence around their garden with used gill net, and it was fairly effective. "But the deer chewed a few holes in the fence and each time, the damage they did overnight was unbelievable." The deer nuzzled heads of lettuce and nibbled out the tender leaves at the heart. They tested the green beans and the peas, but like the customers on Spring Street, the deer's favorite crop was the sweet corn.

"Here it comes!" someone would always say when the farm truck became visible on the main road into town. "It" was, of course, the corn. As the truck and the trailer full of corn pulled up in front of the store, the little crowd often cheered, and immediately a line would form. One Saturday, a woman had been waiting for a long time to ensure a place at the head of the line when the trailer arrived. She frowned up the street half a dozen times, worrying and waiting. When the truck arrived, she went right to work and counted out a dozen ears. Then, as she approached the card table where the pay station had been set up, she hugged her bag and smiled a big, giddy, uncontrollable smile. Every time I eat corn from Dragonfly Farms, I feel the same way.

These days, Robert Rogers sells his corn at the Saturday farmers' market, and few people realize that he was there before the market ever was. Robert's son and daughter often collect money at the stand. Louisa, the careful gardener who started it all, died some years ago, but she seems to hover in spirit over the corn.

HERB-ROASTED CORN
(serves 6)

>6 ears corn, husked
>3 tablespoons butter or olive oil
>1 tablespoon crushed garlic
>1 teaspoon each dried tarragon, thyme, and
>   basil, or 1 tablespoon each fresh,
>   chopped
>½ teaspoon each salt and ground
>   black pepper

Preheat oven to 400°F. Have ready 6 sheets of baker's parchment, each large enough to wrap an ear of corn. In a small saucepan over medium heat, melt butter or warm olive oil; stir in garlic, herbs, salt, and pepper. When mixture is sizzling, remove from heat.

Place an ear of corn on a piece of baker's parchment, spread about 2 teaspoons of garlic and herb mixture over corn, then wrap parchment up and around ear of corn, twisting ends of parchment to seal. Repeat with remaining ears of corn. Arrange wrapped ears on a baking sheet and roast 15 minutes. Serve hot in paper wrappers.

CORN CHOWDER
(makes about 8 cups, to serve 6)

>4 cups milk
>3 large Yukon Gold or other thin-skinned
>   potatoes
>⅓ pound bacon
>1 large onion, peeled and diced
>4 stalks celery, diced

1 tablespoon chopped garlic
¼ cup flour
6 ears of corn
Salt and pepper to taste
¼ cup chopped parsley

In a large saucepan over medium heat, bring milk to a slow boil, watching closely to keep it from boiling over. Meanwhile, cut potatoes into 1-inch dice. Add diced potatoes to milk and cook 12 to 15 minutes, or just until tender.

Cut bacon across slices into ¼-inch bits, and in a soup kettle over medium-high heat, cook until well browned. With a slotted spoon, lift cooked bacon bits out of the rendered bacon fat and set aside.

Sauté onion, celery, and garlic in bacon fat 5 minutes, or until soft and just beginning to brown. Stir in flour, then stir in a cup of the milk in which potatoes have been cooked. Stir vigorously to prevent lumping. Stir in remaining milk and cooked potatoes.

Reduce heat to medium-low. With a sharp knife, strip kernels from corn and add scraped kernels to soup. Simmer 10 to 15 minutes, then season to taste with salt and pepper.

In a small bowl, combine reserved cooked bacon and chopped parsley. Serve chowder hot with a generous spoonful of bacon and parsley mixture sprinkled over each serving.

*D*uring the third week of August, Henry's lemonade stand—ordinarily a modest little enterprise—suddenly becomes a booming business. "More ice!" he shouts from the front door. "More cookies! Cups! Lemonade!" Business booms because we live just a few blocks from the fairgrounds, and for one week every summer our neighborhood becomes a kind of sideshow. We are on display, and we in turn get to watch the parade of fairgoers.

Teenagers and twenty-somethings dressed in black display dangling silver chains from their various pierced appendages. "How much?" they ask.

"Fifty cents," says my son. Then, pushing for the sale, he adds, "It's organic." The young people count their change. A group of two or three might buy one cup to share.

Carefully groomed older adults dressed in clean pastels walk by. "Can we take your picture?" they want to know, snapping their cameras before he has time to answer. Sometimes they buy cups and cups, and they try the cookies too.

The most regular customer, and the most difficult, is the entrepreneur's own brother, Erich. He buys fractions of a cup for a few pennies and demands to help run the stand. He tells the customers that the stand is his too, and he has to be watched carefully to see that he doesn't drift off the sidewalk and into the street. He justifies his existence by running supplies from the kitchen.

All morning long the fairgoers stroll past our home en route to the fairgrounds. Sometimes, Henry likes to invite a friend or a cousin over to help with the stand. Sometimes sales suffer. The children are too happy playing with one another to push their product. A bored and lonely-looking child evokes a kind of sympathy in potential customers. A pair of lively kids drinking lemonade from their own messy stand evokes something else.

But during fair week, nothing can slow down the sales. Henry and his partners fill cup after cup, dole out cookies, and count their quarters. Early in the afternoon, the kids close up shop and follow the crowd to the fair to spend their profits. They come home filled with corn dogs and cotton candy and sleep like tired soldiers.

"I don't need to go to the fair this year," I said one year. "I can just live vicariously through the kids." And besides, I thought, I have more important things to do.

This was the first year in a long time when I had not displayed any of my own work for the judges. On Tuesday, the last day for entries, my whole family had been stranded in a ferry lane in Anacortes until long after the deadline had passed. With no role in the competition, my enthusiasm was tempered. Besides, I needed to concentrate on my work.

Reports from my wife and kids trickled in about who had entered this and who had entered that, who had won ribbons and who had not. I heard about the carnival rides and all the things for sale. The chicken races were scheduled for Saturday morning.

My coworkers were all abuzz.

"I've decided I just can't make it to the fair this year," I told them, and their collective response was that I was full of it. "You've got to go to the fair," they said.

Saturday dawned cool and gray, and I rose early. I had a few quiet minutes alone. I sipped my coffee and made a "to do" list for the day. In the solitude, a breeze rustled some poppies drying for seed on my back porch, and the rattling shook something inside me awake. It occurred to me that summer was almost over. "Life is going by!" cried my soul. "Don't miss the fair!" I dropped my pen and woke up the boys.

"Come on guys, we're going to the fair!"

"It's not even open yet."

"It will be by the time you get your clothes on and have breakfast!"

"What about the lemonade stand?" they cried. "What about our money?"

"I'll give you all the money you need," I promised recklessly. Then I piled everyone in the car and raced to the bank to cash my paycheck. "So much for the household budget," I thought.

We parked at home and joined throngs of people walking past our house to the fair. As I made my way down the midway, I realized that our fair is a two-sided, slightly schizophrenic affair. On one side lies the carnival, with its colorful rides and its worldly barkers. On the other side it's all locals, the food fair, island businessmen hosting the fund-raising salmon barbecue, the Mellowoods music stage where local musicians become stars for a day.

Somewhere in between, or woven throughout, lies the spirit of the fair. Under the big tin roof of the vast main building, under the various roofs of the animal and woolen barns, and under the open sky of the arena, island artists, homemakers, farmers, and craftspeople display their talents in a unique forum that is neither commercial nor simply competition or performance. It is sharing all that is good and interesting about island life, and about life in general.

The entries are what it's all about. My own success with entries has waxed and waned over the years. I have displayed some embarrassing baked goods and preserves that failed to receive a ribbon even when they were the only entry in their category. But I have had triumphs too. A peach pie once took best of show and earned me a gift certificate to the local grocery store.

My most thrilling accomplishment was my first blue ribbon. Made from a variation on a recipe that used to be printed on the back of the Hershey's chocolate box, my cake had more intense flavor because I replaced the milk with coffee. Milk coats the tongue, or binds with the chocolate, or does something wholesome that interferes with the full expression of chocolate. I also intensified the flavor by using dark brown sugar instead of white.

Since then, I have developed several more formulas for chocolate cake—a fancy truffle cake stacked with chocolate mousse, a cake made with ground almonds and hazelnuts instead of flour, an almost weightless chocolate angel food cake—all of them delightful cakes really, but none of them has captured so sweetly the simple pleasure of this all-American layer cake.

Part of what made my cake worthy of a blue ribbon was a trick I picked up from pastry chefs and restaurant cooks, who pile semi-solids such as meringue, frosting, and mashed potatoes into pastry bags to pipe onto pies, cakes, or dinner plates. The same trick can be easily performed at home with an ordinary plastic self-sealing food storage bag. Fill the bag with frosting or meringue and snip a 1-inch piece from one corner of the bag. Squeeze frosting through the hole instead of spreading with a spatula or a knife. No pressure is applied to the cake below, so there is no crumbling, and the results mark the difference between a cake that's merely good and one that's worthy of a blue ribbon.

BLUE RIBBON CHOCOLATE CAKE
(makes one 9-inch layer cake)

> 2½ ounces unsweetened chocolate
> ¾ cup unsalted butter, softened
> 2 cups brown sugar
> 2 eggs
> 2¼ cups flour
> 1 teaspoon baking soda
> ½ teaspoon salt
> 1⅓ cups brewed coffee
> 1 teaspoon vanilla extract
> Chocolate Frosting (recipe follows)

Have all ingredients at room temperature. Preheat oven to 350°F. Grease and flour two 9-inch cake pans, preferably ones with removable bottoms. In a double boiler or a stainless steel bowl, set over a pan of barely simmering water, melt chocolate and set aside.

In a large mixing bowl, whisk butter with brown sugar until very smooth and fluffy. Add eggs, one at a time, beating well after each addition. Stir in melted chocolate. In a separate bowl, whisk together flour, baking soda, and salt.

Whisk about ¾ cup of the flour mixture into the butter mixture, then whisk in ½ cup of the coffee. Add another ¾ cup flour mixture and another ½ cup coffee, stirring well after each addition. Stir in remaining flour mixture, remaining coffee, and vanilla extract.

Transfer batter to prepared cake pans and bake 25 to 30 minutes, or until cake springs back when pressed lightly in the center. Cool cake on racks before removing from pans. Place one cake round on a cake plate and cover with a third of the frosting. Top with second cake layer. Pile half the remaining frosting into a self-sealing food storage bag and snip a 1-inch piece from one corner. Pipe frosting onto sides of cake in even, overlapping stripes to completely cover the sides. Refill the impromptu pastry bag with the remaining frosting and cover the entire surface of the cake with fanciful whirls to give the cake an impressive-looking finish.

CHOCOLATE FROSTING
(makes about 3 cups, to fill and cover one 2-layer cake)

> *4 tablespoons (½ stick) butter*
> *4½ ounces unsweetened chocolate*
> *5 cups powdered sugar*
> *½ cup plus 1 or 2 tablespoons coffee*

In a double boiler or a stainless steel bowl set over a pan of barely simmering water, melt butter and chocolate. Measure 4 cups of powdered sugar into a large mixing bowl and stir in melted butter and chocolate. Stir in ½ cup coffee. Stir in remaining 1 cup powdered sugar and just enough coffee to make a smooth frosting. Pipe or spread onto cooled cake.

My first summer in Washington was one of open-mouthed awe. Blackberries were everywhere. The abundance was amazing enough, but the indifference of the locals was inconceivable. Couldn't they see the berries? I spent glorious afternoons filling every container I could find. My small apartment in Bellingham was full to the rafters with pans of cobbler, jars of preserves, and vats of wine. For several weeks, I picked berries almost every day. I was like a man possessed. My arms were covered with scratches, my countertops were stained purple, and my refrigerator was overflowing.

I still find it hard to sit still when the blackberries are ripening. I feel compelled to bake something with them, to preserve them, to get the little jewels into jars. I have other feelings too. The blackberries ripen too quickly. I cannot gather them all. Some years I am so busy that I do not gather even enough to make a single pie.

A blackberry is a fine and noble thing, but it is a portent too, an omen, a harbinger, a sign. When the blackberries come, you can be sure that summer will soon be gone. Their color is the color of mourning, their perfume the balm of the shroud. Every berry that falls is another sign of summer's passing.

"What?" you say, "It's only August, why is he mourning summer while she's still in her prime?"

I can't help myself. I mourn all summer long. Even as I stand with my back to the sun, gathering berries on the south-facing side of the vines, I feel the chill, dark air that lies under the vines, and I know that winter winds will blow too soon and that only frozen berries will be around at Christmas. The cool, dry autumn days will drink the juice from some of those plump berries before they're ripe, and some part of me will be dried up too.

It seems odd to me that this bittersweet reminder of summer's passing, the Northwest's quintessential symbol of summer, is not a native. Of course, the West Coast does have a blackberry. "The small coast trailing berry, with its sweet-tart flavor," my friend Sharon Kramis once described it. She was born in the Northwest and relates to the fragile little native berry that was born here too. The local fruit is represented in my neighborhood by a secret low-growing vine that narrowly escaped the bulldozers last spring and bears just enough berries to brighten a walker's mouth. There are not enough to gather any serious amount.

I identify with the less-desirable towering Himalayan, the newcomer, which, according to Kramis, "is juicy and seedy," and spreads like wildfire wherever it is allowed to sink its tenacious roots, spreads like the new settlers who crowd the cities of the modern Northwest, transforming it from a string of charming backwater towns along the coast into a vast megalopolis roughly the shape of the freeway. I know these blackberries are no more native than the Scandinavian families who came to Seattle a hundred years ago or the French traders who worked for the Hudson's Bay Company a hundred years before that, but the towering canes have woven themselves into the fiber of the region, and for a late-comer like me they might as well have been here all along.

The ripening blackberries remind me that time is possessed of a current, that we are all caught up in it, and that none of us will be here forever. So while the berries are still on the vine, I will gather as many as I can. At the table with my family, I will let ice cream melt over sweet blackberry crisp. If I have enough time, some of the berries will be made into jam, to be spread eventually over toasted homemade bread in winter.

A few may even become what used to be called a cordial, a sweet alcoholic drink that sends its consumers into a nostalgic reverie when it is sipped after dinner in front of the fire. When autumn comes, my berries will stay plump in a brandy bath, so that in winter I may sip the dregs of summer and watch the vines for signs of spring.

If you are planning to make jam, choose berries that are slightly underripe. Before they have completely ripened, berries contain a starch called pectin that bonds with sugar and water and causes the jam to jell. If the fruit becomes overripe, some of the pectin will have begun to deteriorate, and your jam may not set. Fully ripe or even slightly overripe berries do make excellent cordials.

BLACKBERRY CORDIAL
(makes about 3 pints)

>   1 quart ripe blackberries, crushed
>   1 cinnamon stick
>   1 quart brandy or vodka
>   1 cup sugar, or to taste

In a clean 2-quart jar with a close-fitting lid, pile blackberries and add cinnamon stick and brandy or vodka. Allow berries to stand for at least 2 weeks, turning the jar every other day or so to distribute contents evenly.

After 2 weeks or more, strain liquid through a fine-mesh strainer into a clean jar and stir in sugar. (Don't fuss around, because while the liquid is uncovered, some of the alcohol will evaporate.) For a very clear cordial, allow the liquid to stand undisturbed in a covered jar for a full day and then siphon it gently off the top into a separate container. If you can be content with cordial that is less than perfectly clear, skip that step.

Transfer finished cordial to clean, fancy bottles. (Recycled 375-milliliter wine bottles are ideal.) Seal the bottles with new corks that have been soaked in boiling water for 2 or 3 minutes to render them supple. (Corks can be purchased at winemaking supply stores and at some hardware stores.) If the corks do not go all the way into the bottle, don't worry; just push them in as far as you can.

PACIFIC BLACKBERRY JAM
(makes 5½ pints, plus a little extra)

> *4 cups (tightly packed) blackberries*
> *½ cup lemon juice*
> *4 cups sugar*

In a stockpot or a canning kettle, cover 6 clean 8-ounce canning jars with boiling water. Simmer, covered, over low heat while jam is prepared.

In a clean, dry 4-quart soup kettle over high heat, mash berries with lemon juice. When mixture comes to a full, rolling boil, stir in sugar all at once. Continue stirring until mixture returns to a boil, then insert a candy thermometer. Stir gently until thermometer registers 220°F, or until the jam passes the "sheeting test." (Before it reaches the jelling point, jam runs off the back of a spoon in two distinct streams; as soon as it is ready, the streams will come together to form one. Just as the two streams are joined, a small but plainly visible "sheet" forms between them.)

Remove cooked jam from the stove and set aside. With tongs, lift sterilized jars from simmering water bath and arrange on a clean kitchen towel. Using a canning funnel, or pouring carefully from the kettle, transfer jam to sterilized jars, leaving ½-inch headspace. Seal jars according to manufacturer's instructions, then return jam-filled jars to boiling water bath and boil 5 minutes. Using special tongs or ordinary tongs and a kitchen towel, remove jam jars from boiling water bath and allow to cool undisturbed for several hours or overnight. Check lids to make sure jars have sealed; any that fail to seal should be refrigerated. Sealed jam keeps in a cool, dark place for at least one year.

fall

We should find a house in town," reasoned Betsy. "That way, if the car breaks down, we can walk to work." We knew it was time to move out of the tiny guest cottage beside her parents' vacation house on Brown Island, but we weren't sure we were ready to commit to a life in the islands.

We had come to Friday Harbor with the intention of staying for just a few months to plan our future, but had settled inadvertently at the guest cottage. Graduate school was discussed, but I was half-hearted in my pursuit of a career in public health, and the graduate exams collected dust on a shelf while we fell into the rhythms of island living. Our first season stretched almost imperceptibly into two. Then, having endured the fall and winter, we felt justified in squatting through spring and summer.

Now it was fall again and we realized that we had been in the islands for a full year. It was time to move out of the guest cottage and find a place of our own. I consulted the newspaper.

"This one sounds good," I said, reading only the monthly rates. "And so does this one."

"We'll never find a rental in the newspaper," said the wiser member of the family, but she agreed to come along and have a look. At each site we visited, I said, "This one will do." I was still thinking of our island sojourn in very temporary terms.

"Let's keep looking," she said, even when we had visited every advertised place in town—except one. It was not listed with a local agent, and the landlords had not returned our call.

"What do you expect us to do, just walk through the neighborhood you like and find an empty house?" That was precisely what she expected, and at the dead end of Franck Street, her favorite street in town, an apparently abandoned house peered out of the woods.

There were no curtains in the windows, and the driveway was overgrown with weeds. Through the windows, we could see knotty pine paneling, a fireplace, and a stairway leading up to the second floor. There was a tiny kitchen with buckled yellow Formica countertops and appliances that looked like something from the set of *Leave It to Beaver*.

"It's perfect," she said. A week later we were painting the upstairs rooms, replacing the Formica with sand-colored tiles, and installing a light fixture on the bare bulb that hung from the living room ceiling.

We moved in on Halloween in 1986 with a dog, a cat, a goldfish, and a canary. We had a futon, a few boxes of books, and a few scraps of furniture left from our college days. When we moved out, nine years later to the day, we had a new dog, two cats, three goldfish, a parakeet, two little boys, a moving van full of furniture, and at least a thousand books, even after giving about that many to the library.

At first we thought of the Franck Street house as our honeymoon cottage. Deep green woods came right up to the door. A moss-covered hill behind the house was crowned with blackcap vines and flanked with mushroom-filled woods. By the time we moved out, two houses and a set of condominiums had replaced the trees, and a spectacular view over the rooftops revealed the harbor, the ferry lanes, and snow-covered Mount Baker beyond.

Every Halloween, on the anniversary of our moving in, we filled the driveway with paper bag lanterns and watched the trick-or-treaters find their way to our door. Every Easter we planted colored eggs and candy amid the English daisies for our children and our friends' children to find.

When I calculate how many meals we must have eaten on the lawn with the mountain in the background, or in the tiny kitchen with the bird feeder outside the window, the numbers are staggering. One day, during the week when we moved out, I looked around the tiny kitchen and living room filled with boxes of books and dishes, the rolled-up rug, and the mismatched chairs, and all I could see were the memories. My newborn son would forever be bathing in that sink, laughing out loud under a head full of shampoo. Our old English sheepdog would forever hurry over the slippery kitchen floor for his last car ride. The newlywed kisses, Henry's and Erich's first steps, the candlelit dinners, and the preschool breakfasts formed a collage of images that time would never erase.

How many loaves of homemade bread did we pull out of that oven? Did we really have dinner guests cramped around that tiny table? Did the long, long brown couch from my in-laws' summer home really fit under that window, and what's become of it now? Did we really complain that the house wasn't big enough when we outgrew it? Stumbling as we did into one of the most beautiful situations imaginable, I think we had more blessings there than we will ever be able to count. Nevertheless, I try to count them anyway.

At least a thousand different dinners were prepared in the Franck Street house, and some were better than others. But when I think of that kitchen, I think of roasted chicken with garlic mashed potatoes. Dappled light pours in through the windows, and the open oven takes the edge off the ever-present chill in the air. In the early years, we cooked the potatoes and garlic together in one pot and mashed them together. Toward the end of our sojourn there, we cooked the garlic in a separate pot because the kids preferred their mashed potatoes plain.

ROAST CHICKEN WITH HERBS
(serves 4)

> *1 chicken (4 pounds), preferably free-range*
> *1 tablespoon kosher salt*
> *2 teaspoons dried thyme leaves*
> *1 teaspoon dried sage*
> *1 teaspoon freshly ground black pepper*
> *Sprigs of fresh thyme and sage (optional)*
> *1 can (17 ounces) chicken broth, or 2 cups homemade*
> *2 tablespoons cornstarch, or ¼ cup flour*

Preheat oven to 350°F, and position rack near center. Place chicken in a 6-cup oval ceramic baking dish or a 9-by-13-inch baking pan, then sprinkle inside and out with kosher salt, dried herbs, and pepper. If you like, place a few sprigs of each herb inside the cavity of the chicken. Roast 90 minutes, basting from time to time if desired.

Transfer chicken from pan to a carving board or a platter. Tilt the roasting pan over a cup to collect pan drippings, and set aside. (Fat will rise to the surface and flavorful juices will sink to the bottom.) Pour 1 cup chicken broth into the roasting pan. With a metal spatula, scrape up any bits clinging to the pan. In a small saucepan over medium-high heat, whisk cornstarch or flour into remaining cup of chicken broth and cook, stirring constantly, until mixture begins to boil. Stir in broth from roasting pan and continue stirring until boiling and slightly thickened. Discard most of fat from the top of reserved pan drippings, then whisk juices into sauce. Transfer sauce to a gravy boat. Serve chicken hot with garlic mashed potatoes, a simple green vegetable, and the sauce.

GARLIC MASHED POTATOES
(makes about 4 cups)

> *4 cups water*
> *2 pounds baking potatoes, peeled and cut*
> *into 1-inch chunks*
> *1 head garlic, broken into cloves and peeled*
> *2 tablespoons olive oil*
> *1 teaspoon salt, or to taste*

In a large saucepan over high heat, bring 3 cups water to a boil. Add potatoes, cover, and reduce heat to medium-low. Cook covered, 12 to 15 minutes, or until soft. In a separate pan over high heat, bring remaining 1 cup water and garlic to a boil. Cover, reduce heat to low, and cook 12 to 15 minutes, or until fork-tender. Using the lid of the pan to prevent potatoes from tumbling out, drain water from cooked potatoes into another pot or a heatproof measuring cup. With a sturdy wire whisk or a potato masher, crush the potato chunks. Add just enough reserved cooking liquid to crushed potatoes to make a fairly smooth purée. In a blender, purée cooked garlic with olive oil and enough reserved cooking liquid to a very smooth consistency. Stir into mashed potatoes. Add salt to taste and serve at once.

know a place where there are apple trees a hundred years old and the apples are the best you'll ever eat," claimed my friend Sylvia.

"Take me there!" I said. I had been complaining that apples from the store lacked the substance and character to make really good pies. A few days later we were hiking through the woods with baskets and backpacks, crossing a wide, open field toward what looked like an impenetrable patch of brambles.

"They're right back here." And there they were. Old, noble trees with limbs that blended invisibly into gnarled trunks rose from a tangle of blackberry vines and wild roses reaching almost as high as the trees themselves. We boosted one another up and around the prickly vines until we had footholds in the trees.

Huge, hard apples with cheeks just beginning to blush were everywhere, and their fragrance was so powerful that I could smell them as soon as I saw them. They might have been Newtown Pippins, apples so fine that Queen Victoria lifted a ban on American-grown fruit so that she could import them to England. Or they might have been a variety that islanders call "eighteen-ouncers." In any case they were big, powerful apples.

They were apples so firm that they would bake into a pie you could slice piping hot. Other apple pies will go to pieces and run everywhere if you try to slice the pie before it cools, but a pie made from these apples is more substantial, neither too dry nor too juicy, simply perfect.

We left the woods with our baskets and backpacks loaded with apples, laughing in the yellow-leaf sunlight, happy as children.

"I already have more apples than I know what to do with," said Sylvia, "but I want to see these on my kitchen counter when the afternoon sun comes pouring in."

The next year when the apples began to ripen, Sylvia was ill. A virulent form of cancer was tearing through her body. By the time she knew what was happening, it was too late. The medical professionals were willing to try anything, but they made it clear that the cancer was not likely to respond to treatment.

Rather than subject herself to a battery of radiation and chemicals that to her seemed to promise only complication and institutionalization, Sylvia bravely chose to spend her last few weeks in the home of some friends with whom, ironically, she had planned to open a kind of healing center.

Many of us who loved her felt that she should at least try the conventional route. But Sylvia was a born nonconformist, a sparkling artist whose passion for design and beauty led her through a successful career in the textile industry and eventually to this beautiful orchard-covered island where, with her husband, she had a few bright, wonderful years. She had wanted to get out of the city, and the San Juan Islands are as out of the city as she could get.

I went back to that orchard while Sylvia lay dying and picked her some apples. I wanted her to experience again, at least in her mind, the joy of harvesting fruit from those ancient trees. It was too early in the season, and the apples weren't as ripe as they should have been, but I felt some urgency. I wanted her to taste those apples and imagine how they had hung from their branches beneath the clear autumn sky.

I called the house where she was staying. I spoke to her husband and he told me that Sylvia, barely forty years old, could no longer eat apples. "Maybe I can make her some applesauce," he said, trying to offer me some comfort, trying to hold on to some sense of normalcy.

The next year, when the apples were ripe, I went again to that decaying orchard in the woods and looked at the bright blue autumn sky, felt the cool breeze competing with the sunshine in the battle between the seasons, and heard the leaves rustling through the motions of their little dance that would end with the first stiff wind of winter.

I felt the tenuous hold that all of us have on life, and I showed Henry the trees. He was only a baby then, but already he loved life and he loved apples. I picked one and offered it to him. He ate happily. I took off my shirt and made it into a kind of basket to carry more apples. When my wife put her arm around me and our little family moved from the orchard into the open field, I could almost feel Sylvia smiling on us, knowing that she had led us to this spot where the trees are a hundred years old and the apples are the best I've ever eaten.

Now Henry and his little brother follow me to the orchard every year. I have never told them why I like to gather apples at this particular orchard. There are more accessible trees, and we now have in our own backyard a large and wonderful old apple

141

tree that bears apples much like these. The boys have never asked why we go there either; they accept our annual visit to the apple trees as an adventure, and they await the perfect apple pie that inevitably follows.

Many apples that taste great fresh are poor baking apples. Of the varieties most commonly available, Golden Delicious is probably the best choice for pie; Granny Smiths are a good second choice. Newtown Pippins, sometimes seen in supermarkets, are really excellent for pie. Do not use Red Delicious, Fuji, or Gala for baking.

CLASSIC APPLE PIE
(makes one 10-inch pie, to serve 8)

> Perfect Butter Pastry (recipe follows)
> ¾ cup sugar
> ¼ cup flour
> ¼ cup butter, melted
> 1 to 2 tablespoons lemon juice
> 1 teaspoon ground cinnamon
> 6 or 7 Newtown Pippin or Golden Delicious
>   apples

Preheat oven to 325°F. Line a 10-inch pie pan with half the butter pastry. Keep the other round of pastry cool. In a mixing bowl, combine sugar, flour, melted butter, lemon juice, and cinnamon.

Peel the apples with a potato peeler, cut them into quarters, and remove the cores. In a food processor fitted with a ⅛-inch slicing blade, or with a sharp knife, thinly slice the apples. Toss sliced apples with sugar mixture to coat, then pile mixture into pastry-lined pan. Place second round of dough over filling and fold edges together to seal. With a sharp paring knife, cut several 1-inch slits in top crust to allow steam to escape during baking. Bake 1 hour. Cool completely before slicing.

PERFECT BUTTER PASTRY
(makes enough for 1 double-crust pie)

> 2¼ cups flour
> 1 cup cold butter, cut into bits
> ⅓ cup cold water

In a food processor or a mixing bowl, combine flour and butter and process or work with a fork until mixture is uniformly crumbly. Add water all at once and pulse the food processor motor or stir with a fork to form a dough. Do not overmix, or dough will be become elastic and pastry will be tough. Divide dough in half. On a floured work surface, roll each piece of dough into a 12-inch circle. Chill rolled pastry until ready to use.

I walk into the kitchen and open a cabinet as quietly as I can, trying not to attract any attention. I carefully remove a mixing bowl and place it silently on the countertop. I turn on the oven and pull out the muffin tin. A pan rattles. I turn my head toward the door. Sure enough, they heard it. Before I can blink, my three-year-old, Erich, is dragging out the stepping stool, and Henry, the seven-year-old, is sidling up to the counter between me and the mixing bowl to make sure he doesn't miss a beat.

"What you making, DaDa?" Erich wants to know. "Can we help?" asks Henry. Soon they're cracking eggs, stirring things up, and competing for access to the bowl. "Not too much baking powder!" I shout from the sidelines. "Wait to add the milk!"

Sometimes, I manage to get the muffin tins buttered and floured or the dry ingredients stirred together before the helpers descend. Usually not. They are quicker than I am.

The great challenge of cooking for kids is, of course, cooking with kids, but this is paradoxically also the great reward. Teaching children to cook is more gratifying than teaching them to dress themselves or to wash behind their ears. I like to imagine that we will cook together as long as they live at home, and these shared times will resonate in our kitchens and our minds long after they have moved away.

Whenever I begin a stew by browning flour in oil, I am transported to my mother's side thousands of miles away, and I hear her voice shape the word "roux" in the warm southern diction of the Gulf Coast where I spent my childhood. Even though we are on opposite sides of the continent, we are together at the stove.

When I am kneading bread or stirring batter, I see my children's efforts to imitate mine, and I know that I will never do it alone again without remembering these hectic days of flour in the air and on the floor, of milk splashed everywhere and eggshells pulled agonizingly out of gooey batters. "When I'm old and lonely," I tell myself, "I'll be glad I did this."

But cooking together provides more than memories, binding family members through time and space. Learning to make everyday dishes like muffins or soup or rice and vegetables is not only fun for kids, it's invaluable, and the knowledge gained in the kitchen has ripples that expand to every area of life.

Yeast dough rising in a bowl exposes little minds to a whole world of unseen life forms. My boys knead dough with the practiced hands of master bakers, and they understand that while they watch cartoons or play on their swing set, the yeasts are growing and "breathing into the dough."

"They're little tiny animals, you know," Henry tells Erich as granules of active dry yeast rain down on a bowl of warm water. Erich sprinkles while Henry stirs.

When I was a child, the kitchen was not so much a biology lab as it was a social studies book. I learned as much about geography from the Time-Life Foods of the World series as I ever did in geography class. M.F.K. Fisher's volume on provincial France was a portrait of a people and their land as much as it was of their

145

food, and a gingerbread house from the volume on Germany helped me see the brighter side of a country that I had previously seen only in old war movies.

The most valuable cooking lessons of all transcend mere technical skills and resonate in a metaphorical zone where all sorts of learning takes place in a Robert Fulghum kind of world where kindergarten never ends. "Wait until the pancake is covered with bubbles before you flip it. . . . Even though it's fun to sprinkle, use only a little salt, or you'll ruin the corn." These are the almost painfully obvious lessons in the virtues of patience and simplicity.

But all of this is peripheral. The real point of cooking for children, the primary goal, with or without their assistance, is to make something wholesome that they will eat. Children are instinctively dubious about trying new foods and are almost invariably opposed to eating anything having what an adult would call "real flavor."

Even if you manage to stay sane and calm while your youngsters are helping you cook, and even if you have chosen a menu that will tempt their budding palates, food prepared for children may not be appetizing to you. At our house, the adults like spicy foods, but the children tend to like plain foods, very plain.

"To their pure, unadulterated palates, things taste more intense," wrote the late novelist and *Gourmet* columnist Laurie Colwin. "Which explains why children seem to like things one at a time (the squash here, the bread there, the noodles there) as opposed to combinations such as lasagna." But to jaded old palates like mine, things like mashed potatoes and buttered noodles taste intensely bland. So we have found ways to bring simple nursery foods and the explosive spice-infused dishes our ancient palates demand to the same table.

Fish fillets are broiled plain. Half receive a sprinkle of salt and a dab of butter, perfect for kids. The other half get brushed with a mixture of lemon zest, garlic, chopped parsley, lemon juice, and olive oil. "Please don't put any of that on mine," begs Henry, his face contorted into an awful grimace.

At breakfast, though, we all like the same things, and one of those things is waffles. Whenever we have a little extra time to make something special, or when we run out of cereal and cannot face a pre-coffee trip to the store, we make waffles. Our favorite waffle recipe allows for buckwheat flour when we have it but works fine with whole wheat or even all white. If you do not have a waffle iron, do not despair. This same formula works well for pancakes.

Since we often discover that we're out of maple syrup just about the time the waffles are ready, we have devised a formula for our own quick brown sugar syrup that works very well. If you have corn syrup, a half cup will give the syrup extra body; it will also prevent the syrup from crystallizing if you plan to save the leftovers.

GOLDEN WAFFLES
(makes 4 large waffles)

> 1 cup all-purpose flour
> 1 cup buckwheat flour or whole wheat flour
> 1 tablespoon baking powder
> 1 teaspoon salt
> 3 eggs
> 2 tablespoons sugar
> ⅓ cup vegetable oil

1½ cups milk
Maple syrup or Quick Brown Sugar Syrup
(recipe follows)

Preheat a waffle iron. In a large mixing bowl, combine the flours well with the baking powder and salt.

In a smaller bowl, lightly beat the eggs. Whisk in sugar and oil, then stir in the milk and add this mixture all at once to the flour mixture, stirring just until all ingredients are combined. Butter the iron and, using about ¾ cup of the batter at a time, bake waffles according to iron manufacturer's instructions, or until the waffles are crisp and golden. Serve with maple syrup or Quick Brown Sugar Syrup.

QUICK BROWN SUGAR SYRUP
(makes about 2 cups)

2 cups brown sugar
1 cup water
Pinch salt
½ cup corn syrup (optional)

In a saucepan over high heat, stir together brown sugar, water, and salt. Bring the mixture to a boil, then remove from heat and stir in corn syrup, if desired. Serve warm or hot with waffles or pancakes.

One of the nicest things about living on an island is going off island. This is not to say I don't like living on an island. I like it very much, and yet there is something exhilarating about driving onto a ferryboat and leaving the island behind. I have always loved going somewhere, going anywhere, and a ferry ride that lasts for well over an hour leaves no doubt that one has gone somewhere.

Before I started traveling to the city regularly, I went to the mainland less than once a month. I wondered what it must be like for people who commute by ferry. Would the ferries lose their charm? Would the mainland seem mundane? Now my work takes me to Seattle on a regular basis, and the ferries are as fun as they ever were.

No matter how often I travel, the ride is beautiful. The boats have a romantic, faraway feel that doesn't wear out. Some islanders call going to the mainland "Going to America." America, the mainland, with its freeways and shopping malls, is where I came from, but it is also, in a way, a place from which I escaped. When my work there is done, I always appreciate coming home again.

Coming or going from the island to the city, the highlight of my trip is usually the trek through Skagit Valley. Betsy and I have always felt that if for any reason we were to leave the island, we would try to go no farther than the Skagit. Over the years, those fields and the way they change through the seasons have become our calendar, our book of days.

In the spring they are covered with their famous tulips. People come from all over the world to walk in the fields and take pictures. In summer they are working fields full of produce and pickers.

In fall, surrounded by trees wearing yellow leaves and red hawthorn berries, the fields begin to shed their growth. Beneath the boiling gray clouds of a low pressure system or the achingly clear blue of a high, the earth is mostly bare, dotted here and there with swollen yellow cucumbers left behind by the harvesters, or bits of pumpkins that lie crushed in the wake of invisible tractors, ready to be reabsorbed by the soil. A few of the fields are covered in purple cabbages, crimson beet greens, or dark green vetch, more vibrant in the failing light of autumn.

Soon the fields and most of the trees around them will be bare, and the dark green firs will be black and menacing against the winter sky. But even when the air is frozen and ice is all around, some of those bare branches will turn red. Long before the buds of spring appear, the willow stems will be yellow against the river. Fall always blends subtly into spring in western Washington, and spring seems to begin before winter even has a foothold.

I stop each week at one of the farms where brussels sprouts, carrots, cabbages, and beets are for sale and farm-fresh potatoes, yellow, red, and blue, are not to be resisted. Even after the corn and squash and greens are gone and the drainage ditches along the sides of the road are filled with ice, these late-season vegetables are still around. When I am careful, I can store enough of those great roots to last all winter. The potatoes will keep if they stay cool and in the dark, and I have secret corners where the conditions are just right. The carrots and beets seem to demand refrigeration, but some of them can be kept by pickling. Then, every time I see them in their jars, I will be reminded of the colors of the valley in autumn.

Carrot pickles have an old-fashioned flavor that seems to cry out for bread and cheese. If the bread is a rustic whole-grain loaf and the cheese is mild and smooth, like Tillamook cheddar from the Oregon coast, then a glass of beer or a sparkling cider can turn the whole affair into an hearty ploughman's lunch. Beetroot purée is one of those vegetable dishes that surprises people. Its brilliant color is matched by its subtle sweetness, and people who eat it always ask for the recipe.

PICKLED CARROT STICKS
(makes 4 quarts)

> *4 pounds carrots, peeled*
> *3 cups apple cider vinegar*
> *3 cups filtered water*
> *1 cup sugar*
> *1 teaspoon kosher salt*
> *1 bay leaf, broken into 4 pieces*
> *1 teaspoon ground allspice*

Using a mandoline if you have one, or a very sharp knife if you don't, cut carrots into ½-by-4-inch matchsticks; set aside.

In a canning kettle or a stockpot, cover 4 widemouthed quart-size canning jars with boiling water. Simmer, covered, over low heat while the pickles are prepared.

In a saucepan over medium-high heat, combine vinegar, water, sugar, salt, bayleaf, and allspice and bring liquid to a boil; reduce heat to a simmer, and cover. In a large kettle over high heat, bring 4 quarts water to a full, rolling boil. Drop in carrot sticks and cook 1 minute, drain in a colander, then transfer to sterilized canning jars.

Pour spiced vinegar mixture over carrots, dividing spices evenly among the jars and allowing ½-inch headspace at the top of each jar. Seal jars according to manufacturer's instructions and return sealed jars to hot water bath. Simmer 20 minutes; then, using special canning tongs or ordinary tongs and a kitchen towel, remove jars from hot water bath. Cool jars at room temperature for several hours or overnight. Check lids to make sure jars have sealed. Any jars that fail to seal may be kept refrigerated for several months. Sealed jars will keep in a cool, dark place for a year. Serve pickles as a garnish for sandwiches or salads.

BEETROOT PURÉE
(makes about 4 cups)

> *2 pounds beets*
> *¼ cup vegetable oil or ghee (Amber Butter, page 234)*
> *1 large onion, peeled and thinly sliced*
> *¼ cup whipping cream*
> *½ teaspoon each salt and pepper*

Trim beets, leaving 1 inch of stem attached, then cook in boiling water until just tender. (Very large beets may take as long as 45 minutes to cook; smaller ones may be done in 20 minutes.) While beets are cooking, heat vegetable oil or ghee in a sauté pan over

medium-high heat and sauté sliced onion until very soft and beginning to brown. Transfer sautéed onion to a blender and set
aside. Drain beets and, under cold running water, slip off skins.
Cut into 2-inch chunks and add to blender with cream and seasonings. Purée until smooth. Purée may be kept hot in the top of
a double boiler.

*L*ong before I came to the Pacific Northwest, I knew about the mushrooms here. I was a college student when I read Tom Robbins's book *Another Roadside Attraction,* and I fell under the spell of the fictional character Amanda, who personified the fertile Skagit Valley. She languished in the "mashed banana sunlight of Labor Day afternoon" and dreamed of ways to serve her favorite food, forest mushrooms.

Not long after I moved to Bellingham, at the northern end of Skagit Valley, I attached myself to a little knot of mushroom hunters and tagged along with them into the woods, where I gathered my first chanterelles and tasted the thrill of the hunt that has never left me. Now, every fall, when the leaves are the golden color of chanterelles, Betsy and I take to the woods with our children in tow and forage for the handful of familiar varieties of mushrooms we know well enough to bring to the table.

When they were too young to walk, the boys rode in a backpack. Now they run ahead and lag behind, as wild as the mushrooms, and although their ages combined only make ten, they can already identify chanterelles. The chanterelle is a family favorite, but we also love the common field mushroom (*Agaricus campestris*) and its royal cousin The Prince (*Agaricus augustus*).

Along forest paths, in nooks behind our woodpiles, in earthen driveways, and in the middle of our lawns, wild mushrooms sprout with abandon. Tall shaggy manes (*Coprinus comatus*), unmistakable in their flaky coats, rise predictably along a familiar roadside. On a certain trail where we go to see wild lilies in the spring, I keep my eyes peeled in the fall for the squat Zeller's boletus (*Boletus zelleri*), with its colorful spongy caps. Mysterious wood blewits (*Lepista nuda*) occupy a tomato patch my neighbor built with old truck tires, and a nun who lives on Shaw Island once confided in me that she uses young puffballs (*Bovista pila*) instead of meatballs in her spaghetti sauce.

We're still on the lookout for the elusive King Boletus (*Boletus edulis*), hailed as porcini in Italy and as cèpe in France. The famous matsutake (*Tricholoma ponderosum*), also known as the Japanese pine mushroom, eludes me as well. I've never gathered either one, but my fellow fungophiles have, so I know they're out there.

For those who hunt mushrooms in the wild, an experienced companion is invaluable, and a well-illustrated field guide is mandatory. But anyone more interested in cookbooks than in field guides will be happy to know that good mushroom hunting can be done in the local supermarket. Thanks to the efforts of a burgeoning class of professional foragers and mushroom cultivators, wild and cultivated forest mushrooms are sprouting at produce stalls.

Excellent oyster mushrooms and perfect shiitake can be had year-round, and from September until December chanterelles, porcupine mushrooms, and the occasional matsutake can be found in better grocery stores. Under the fluorescent lights of a supermarket, wild fungi look a little naked and pale, rather like E. T. when he's being examined by physicians in white, but once you get them in your kitchen, forest mushrooms come back to life with all the magic of the woodlands.

Tom Robbins, the man who created Amanda and first whetted my appetite for wild mushrooms, came to the island one year to celebrate the wedding of some mutual friends. It was October, and I was in charge of food for the occasion, so of course forest mushrooms were the star attraction. I made a savory stew of several varieties and served the stew in individual whole wheat pastry shells. I liked the filling for those forest mushroom barquettes so much that it became a recurring theme of my autumn kitchen. Here the same basic stew fills a savory variation on Napoleons. Puff pastry sheets may be purchased frozen. When just one kind of mushroom, the lovely chanterelle, is to be found, I like to bake it with chicken.

FOREST MUSHROOM NAPOLEONS
(makes 12 pastries)

> *1 sheet puff pastry, about 10 by 12 inches*
> *1 egg, lightly beaten*
> *Ragout of Forest Mushrooms (recipe follows)*
> *Italian parsley, for garnish*

Preheat oven to 400°F, and place the pastry sheet on a parchment-lined baking sheet. Brush the pastry with beaten egg and score the top with shallow cuts on a 45-degree angle, about ½ inch apart. Cut the pastry into 6 rectangular pieces. Bake 12 to 15 minutes, or until puffed and golden brown. Cool the pastries on a rack. (Pastries my be baked ahead up to this point and kept at room temperature until serving time. If prepared more than a few hours in advance, pastries should be recrisped in a hot oven for 1 minute before filling.)

At serving time, split each pastry in half horizontally, remove the top, and fill with about ½ cup mushroom ragout. Replace the top layer of pastry. Garnish with flat-leafed Italian parsley and serve at once.

A RAGOUT OF FOREST MUSHROOMS
(makes about 3 cups)

> *½ cup sherry*
> *½ cup whipping cream*
> *¼ cup soy sauce*
> *1 tablespoon chopped garlic*
> *2 tablespoons cornstarch*
> *¼ cup clarified butter or olive oil*
> *½ pound fresh shiitake caps, sliced*
> *½ pound chanterelles, sliced*
> *½ pound oyster mushrooms, sliced*

In a small bowl, combine sherry, cream, soy sauce, garlic, and cornstarch; set aside. Over medium-high heat, warm butter or oil in a very large skillet or two smaller ones. Sauté sliced mushrooms for 5 minutes, tossing or stirring to ensure even cooking. Add the sherry mixture all at once and cook 3 minutes longer, tossing or stirring to prevent sticking. Remove from heat. Spoon the ragout into puff pastry cases for a first course, or serve as a side dish.

BREAST OF CHICKEN BAKED WITH CHANTERELLES AND TOMATOES
(serves 4)

1 pound chanterelles, sliced
4 tablespoons butter
6 small Roma or Saladette tomatoes,
    chopped
4 chicken breast halves, boned, with skin
    left intact
1 teaspoon kosher salt
½ teaspoon freshly ground black pepper
½ cup whipping cream
½ cup white wine
1 pound egg noodles, cooked in boiling
    salted water until just tender

Preheat oven to 425°F. In a sauté pan over medium-high heat, cook mushrooms in butter 5 minutes or until most of the water in them is evaporated. In a 6-cup oval ceramic baking dish or a 9-by-13-inch baking pan, make a bed of sautéed chanterelles and chopped tomatoes. Arrange breasts of chicken, skin side up, in a single layer on top, and sprinkle salt and pepper over all. Bake 15 minutes, or until skins are browned.

Meanwhile, in a saucepan over medium-high heat, boil cream and wine until reduced to ¾ cup, then remove from heat.

With a slotted spoon, lift chicken from pan and transfer to a warm platter or serving plates, and set aside. Add mushrooms, tomatoes, and pan juices to reduced cream mixture and cook, stirring, 2 minutes, or until mixture boils and comes together to form a sauce. Ladle sauce over chicken and serve hot with noodles.

lato had a theory of forms. He said that on some astral-like plane, everything we know exists in a pure, ideal state. I think each of us carries our own customized plane of forms inside our heads. When I think of "milk," for instance, I see the old square bottles that used to be delivered by the milkman. Even though the milkman stopped coming when I was still a preschooler, and we started buying milk in paper cartons, that image was engraved on my budding consciousness and remains the standard, if not exactly the ideal, form. "Milk," said someone holding the bottle, and just like that, milk was forever associated in my mind with the old square bottle.

Similarly, the image of "bread" that I carry to this day is a loaf of Sunbeam brand white bread. The wrapper features the slogan "It's batter whipped," along with a picture of a darling blond girl in a blue dress with puffy sleeves, eating a slice of perfect bread.

I grew up in a time when forms were fairly standardized through mass production. I wonder sometimes what sorts of forms—if any—exist in the minds of my little boys. We live in a world where diversity is the norm, and our bread changes from day to day. Today it may be homemade white bread fashioned roughly after my Sunbeam brand "ideal form." Yesterday it was baguettes from a bakery. Betsy and I ate the crispy crusts; Henry and Erich ate the fluffy centers. Tomorrow it may be tortillas.

Some days our bread is store-bought raisin bread, artificially soft from some sort of commercial dough conditioning that I could never duplicate at home. Very often our bread is a mass-produced imitation of the handcrafted breads of Europe. My wife likes crusty country loaves reminiscent of *pain de campagne,* and she is forever trying out breads that might come close. I am forever baking bread from scratch.

I became a disciple of bread baking as a youngster. A family friend demonstrated the craft and I was hooked at once. Everything about the process I found compelling. I was especially intrigued by yeast. I love the fact that it is alive, and that in the case of dry yeast, it lives in a sort of suspended animation. I find mystery in the very word. "Yeast" is derived from the same Indo-European roots as "ghost," and if the connection seems unclear, consider that yeast brings a limp paste of flour and water to life. As it grows, lives, and breathes, yeast fills the dough with air, causing it to lighten and rise. Spirit, in the old sense, means breath, and yeast is the spirit of bread.

The dough itself can be thought of as a living thing. It has certain needs, but these needs are easily met. Give it moisture and warmth, and your dough will thrive, at least for a while. Eventually, left to its own devices, the yeast will use up all the nutrients in the dough, become sour, and gradually die in its own putrid waste; but long before that happens, you can press the air out of it, or "punch it down," as bakers like to say, and shape it into loaves, or rolls, or the crust for a pizza.

Do not be put off by anything you might have read about

specific temperatures and timing. Yeast can live and do business at any temperature where you can live and work. It is important to note, however, that it slows way down if it gets cold, so unless you have all day, keep your dough fairly warm. But remember that if it gets too hot, it will die, so don't let it touch anything that feels hot against your skin. The temperature of the human body, or slightly cooler, is the ideal temperature for reasonably rapid yeast growth. As for timing, almost anything goes. There is no need to become a slave to the schedule of your dough.

Once you assemble a yeast dough, it needs to spend about an hour in a warm bowl to rise before you shape it into loaves or whatever else you have in mind. After shaping, it should rise again for a few minutes before it goes into the oven. But this rising time is an area where you can claim all sorts of liberties. If you are reading a particularly good book, you may decide that your dough must rise a little longer to develop more character, and read on. If you are desperate to get dinner on the table and after twenty or thirty minutes you think that perhaps the yeast has lived long enough, punch it down and get on with it.

The recipe that follows is a loose framework from which you are encouraged to deviate and upon which you are encouraged to build. I developed the recipe from thin air, long before I had ever actually been to Italy and seen the diversity and complexity of real Italian bread. There, most bakers take time to develop a *biga*, what English bakers call a sponge, before they finish assembling their dough. This just means that before all the flour is added to the yeast and water, a thin, batterlike pre-dough is allowed to rise for a time. That extra step allows the yeast to multiply, and it gives the finished bread more character. It also allows bakers to economize by using less yeast. If you have plenty of time, or if you are using your bread baking to avoid some less desirable task, by all means allow the unfinished dough to rise once before you add all the flour.

Of course, this bread is really no more Italian than a hot dog, but it does go well with Italian food. Once you have a viable yeast dough, it can be shaped, filled, and baked in a number of ways to meet your needs. A few baking options follow the basic formula for dough.

"ITALIAN" BREAD DOUGH
(makes enough for 1 large loaf or 2 pizzas)

> *1 cup warm water*
> *1 package active dry yeast*
> *2½ to 2¾ cups flour*
> *2 teaspoons salt*
> *1 teaspoon sugar*
> *2 tablespoons olive oil*

Pour the warm water into a warm mixing bowl and sprinkle yeast over it. Stir to dissolve. Add 1 cup flour and stir with a wire whisk until thoroughly combined. Whisk in salt, sugar, and olive oil, then add another cup of flour. Exchange the wire whisk for a wooden spoon and mix well. With the wooden spoon or your hands, work in enough remaining flour to form a soft dough. On a lightly floured surface, knead dough by pressing and folding for 5 minutes, or until dough is very smooth and springy. Return dough to bowl, cover with plastic wrap or a clean, damp kitchen towel, and allow to rise in a warm place for 1 hour, or until doubled in bulk.

FOOD PROCESSOR METHOD: In a large measuring cup, dissolve yeast in warm water. In the workbowl of a food processor fitted with a steel blade, place 1 cup of flour. With the motor running, pour in water-yeast mixture and process until smooth. Add salt, oil, and 1 more cup flour and process again until smooth. Add just enough of the remaining flour to form a soft dough that leaves the sides of the workbowl. Transfer dough to a warm, oiled mixing bowl and allow to rise. Don't worry about kneading; the processor takes care of that.

A BRAIDED LOAF
"Italian" Bread Dough (see previous recipe)

Preheat oven to 350°F. Line a jelly roll pan or a cookie sheet with baker's parchment, and set aside. Divide risen bread dough into thirds. On a lightly floured surface, roll each portion of dough into a rope about 12 inches long. Lay ropes of dough alongside one another; then, starting at one end, braid ropes together. Transfer to parchment-lined pan and allow loaf to stand, or "proof," at room temperature for 10 to 15 minutes, or until it has risen to about 1½ times its original size. Bake 40 to 45 minutes, or until crust is well browned and a tap on the loaf yields a hollow sound. Doneness may be tested with a quick-read thermometer; the inside of the loaf should be 200°F.

FOCACCIA (FLAT HERB BREAD)
"Italian" Bread Dough (see earlier recipe)
3 tablespoons good-quality olive oil
2 tablespoons chopped fresh herbs (oregano, basil, rosemary)

1 teaspoon crushed red pepper (optional)
1 teaspoon kosher salt

Preheat oven to 400°F. Spread olive oil on a jelly roll pan and set aside. On a lightly floured surface, roll risen bread dough out into a rectangle roughly the same size as the pan and transfer dough to the pan. Turn the dough over so that top and bottom are lightly coated with oil. Sprinkle on herbs, crushed pepper, if desired, and salt. Bake 15 minutes. Cut or tear into pieces and serve hot or warm.

NEAPOLITAN PIZZA
(makes two 12-inch rounds)

"Italian" Bread Dough (see earlier recipe)
Quick Tomato Sauce (recipe follows)
1½ cups grated mozzarella cheese
½ cup grated Parmesan cheese
12 anchovy fillets (optional)
1 tablespoon dried oregano
¼ cup olive oil

Preheat oven to 400°F. Lightly coat two 10-inch round pizza pans or jelly roll pans with olive oil, then dust heavily with flour and shake off any excess. Divide risen dough in half and roll each half into a 12-inch round (the springy dough will shrink to fit the pans) or into a rough rectangle to fill the jelly roll pans. Place rolled dough on prepared pans. Cover with tomato sauce, then sprinkle ¾ cup mozzarella and ¼ cup grated Parmesan over each pizza. Arrange anchovy fillets over cheese, if desired, and sprinkle on oregano. Drizzle olive oil on top. Bake for 25 minutes, or until crust is lightly browned.

QUICK TOMATO SAUCE
(makes about 3 cups)

> *1 small onion, peeled and thinly sliced*
> *2 tablespoons olive oil*
> *2 tablespoons chopped garlic*
> *1 tablespoon dried oregano*
> *1 tablespoon dried basil*
> *¼ teaspoon ground black pepper*
> *½ cup red wine*
> *1 bay leaf*
> *1 can (28 ounces, about 3 cups) chopped*
> *tomatoes in purée*

In a saucepan over high heat, sauté onion in olive oil 2 minutes, or until just beginning to brown. Add garlic, oregano, basil, and pepper, then stir for a few seconds to coat seasonings with oil. Add wine and bay leaf and allow mixture to boil until wine has evaporated and mixture begins to sizzle. Stir in tomatoes, reduce heat to medium, and cook, stirring, 5 minutes, or until heated through.

When I met Betsy's parents, I tried to keep things in perspective. Just because I was meeting the people who might someday become my in-laws, that was no reason to be nervous. She was, after all, only a girlfriend, and I was just some guy from college she happened to bring home for a visit. There was no reason to feel I had to impress anyone.

Still, no other girlfriend had taken me home to meet her parents, and she let me know that she had introduced them to no other young man in three years of college. A cook at a Mexican restaurant and a student with no clear career goals, I didn't feel like much of a prize, especially when I considered the evidence of the kind of prosperity she had known as a child.

Betsy's parents had a vacation home on Brown Island, a small island in the San Juans, less than a mile from Friday Harbor. There, with one of Betsy's girlfriends along as a chaperone of sorts, we had once spent a few days during spring break and, for some strange reason, had roasted a turkey. In front of a roaring driftwood fire in the oversized fireplace, Betsy had told me about her privileged childhood: a house on Lake Washington, a condo at Crystal Mountain, trips to Europe, to Hawaii. I felt unworthy of trying to provide for her. She deserved so much more than I had to offer.

That I even considered providing a future for her revealed that I was thinking way ahead of myself, but that didn't occur to me then. What had occurred to me from the moment I saw her was that she was unique—possessed of some quality I couldn't name. I wanted to keep looking at her until I could determine just what that something was.

I first saw her over my shoulder, sitting behind me in a lecture hall where we both attended an evening class entitled "Historical Perspectives on Health Education." The class was specifically designed for people who had declared health education as their major, and it was my first opportunity to meet other students in this small and dubiously elect group. The students enrolled in the health program were a mixed bag of physical education majors, frustrated pre-med students attending a university with no pre-med program, and lost souls like Betsy and me who had wandered into the program completely unaware of why we had chosen this particular course of study.

Both of us may have been wondering what we were doing there that evening. The class hadn't quite begun and one of the students, who had apparently appointed herself social director, was inviting us all to a "pizza feed" to be held the following weekend. I had never heard of a feed, pizza or otherwise.

When the social director tapped me on the shoulder and asked if I would like to attend, my first inclination was to burst out laughing, and my second inclination was to find another face to gauge how someone else might respond to this bizarre invitation. My eyes landed on Betsy's, and hers were sparkling with laughter. Eyes fixed on Betsy, unable to look back at the self-appointed social director, I said I would have to check my schedule.

Something in her look was so immediately familiar and new and hypnotic that I spent the rest of the class time obsessing over her. Part of the activities planned for that evening's class included a variation on the game Trivial Pursuit, in which we were to display our knowledge, or lack thereof, in our chosen field. A compulsive retainer of facts, I spewed out answers to every question that was posed, shamelessly flaunting the few wits I possessed, in hopes of impressing Betsy. I was branding myself within the department as a boorish know-it-all, and I knew it. But Betsy, seemingly aware that it was all for her benefit, was amused. After class, I asked if I might walk her home, and within a few weeks came the fateful trip to Brown Island and the out-of-season turkey dinner.

A few months later, when I went to meet Betsy's parents, it was summer, still a long way from fall, and yet we had turkey again. "He likes turkey," Betsy had told her mother. By the time our first Thanksgiving rolled around, and I was eating turkey with Betsy for the third time in one year, we had spent a painfully long summer apart, we had traveled together, she had met my parents, and I had resolved without asking to marry her.

That Thanksgiving was celebrated at the summer house on Brown Island, and several of Betsy's sisters, nieces, and nephews of various ages were gathered for the festivities. As is customary in that family, each person in turn said what they were thankful for, and without hesitation, without even considering the implications, I said that for me it was Betsy.

Now whenever turkey is served or whenever cold winds or bare branches or paper cutouts of pilgrims remind me of Thanksgiving, I think at once of my wife. Even as childhood memories of family gatherings and turkeys past fill my brain, Thanksgiving and turkey are inextricably tied with finding Betsy, meeting her family, and falling in love.

Even if I did not associate it with Betsy, I would say that roasting a turkey is one of the most rewarding experiences a cook can have. It is a time-consuming task but not a tricky one. Turkey is fairly forgiving meat, and successful roasts can be had at oven temperatures ranging from below 300°F to above 400°F. Basting, the practice of ladling some of the pan juices from the bottom of the pan over the top of the bird as it roasts, is a gratifying but optional experience. I always prefer to leave the bird alone in the oven and go for a walk.

Roasting a turkey is pretty much an all-day affair, and lots of leisure time can be woven into the process. The method that follows produces not only a beautiful and delicious dinner but also a day full of wonderful smells and big chunks of time when there is little to do but visit. Serve the roast turkey with mashed potatoes, steamed winter squash, and sautéed kale.

ROAST TURKEY WITH CORNBREAD DRESSING AND MADEIRA GRAVY
(serves 8, with leftovers)

> *1 fresh, natural turkey with giblets (12 to 14 pounds)*
> *2 tablespoons kosher salt*
> *2 tablespoons rubbed (crumbled) sage*
> *1 tablespoon freshly ground black pepper*
> *Cornbread Dressing (recipe follows)*
> *¼ cup flour*
> *1 cup Madeira wine*

Prepare cornbread dressing. Preheat oven to 325°F. Remove giblets from turkey and place neck, heart, and gizzards (but not liver) in a stockpot. Set aside. Sprinkle turkey inside and out with kosher salt, sage, and ground pepper. Pack central cavity and the hollow under the flap of skin at the top of the breast with cornbread dressing. Place stuffed turkey in a large roasting pan. (If your roasting pan has a rack, use it, but this is not essential) Cover turkey with aluminum foil and roast 4 hours (18 to 20 minutes per pound), or until a meat thermometer inserted into a thigh of the bird registers 170°F and juices from the thigh run clear. Remove the foil after 3 hours so that the bird will brown thoroughly during the last hour of roasting.

As soon as the bird goes into the oven, place stockpot containing giblets over medium-high heat and stir until some of the fat is rendered and the skin on neck is beginning to brown. Cover browned giblets with 4 cups water, bring water to a boil, and reduce heat to low. Allow giblet broth to simmer, undisturbed, for 2 to 3 hours, or until the turkey is almost ready.

When the turkey comes out of the oven, allow it to stand for 5 minutes. Then, using the rack if your roasting pan has one or a pair of metal spatulas if it doesn't, carefully transfer the bird from the roasting pan to a platter, cover with foil, and set aside. (The turkey will stay hot for several minutes while you make the gravy.)

Tilt the pan to gather the juices in one corner. The clear liquid that lies on the surface of the pan drippings is pure fat; the brown liquid underneath is flavorful pan juices. Into a measuring cup, carefully pour off as much of the clear fat as you can, saving all the brown juices underneath. Measure the brown pan juices and add enough giblet broth to make 3 cups; set aside.

Place ¼ cup of the turkey fat into a large saucepan, discarding the rest. Place saucepan over medium-high heat, stir in flour and, when the mixture is sizzling and just beginning to brown, whisk in Madeira. Continue whisking until mixture is smooth. Still whisking, add pan juice mixture in a steady stream to make a smooth gravy. Serve at once with roast turkey, dressing, and mashed potatoes.

CORNBREAD DRESSING
(makes about 8 cups, to fill a 12- to 14-pound bird)

> *1 batch Cornbread (recipe follows)*
> *¼ cup butter*
> *1 large yellow onion, peeled and cut into*
>   *¼-inch dice*
> *3 stalks celery, cut into ¼-inch dice*
> *2 large carrots, peeled and cut into ¼-inch*
>   *dice*
> *2 eggs*
> *1 tablespoon rubbed (crumbled) sage*
> *1 teaspoon kosher salt*
> *1 teaspoon freshly ground black pepper*
> *½ teaspoon ground nutmeg*
> *1 cup chicken or turkey broth (optional)*

Prepare cornbread.

Preheat oven to 325°F. Cut cornbread into 1-inch pieces and allow to cool completely. In a large sauté pan over medium-high heat, melt butter. Add diced onion, celery, and carrots. Cook, stirring, until vegetables are soft and beginning to brown; remove from heat. In a large mixing bowl, beat eggs, then stir in sage, salt, pepper, and nutmeg. Stir in sautéed vegetables and cooled corn-bread pieces. Pack the dressing into the open end of the turkey, pressing any extra into the recessed area under the flap of skin at the neck of the bird. Dressing bakes while turkey roasts. To prepare dressing as a side dish for other roasts, such as pork loin, pile it into a greased baking dish and douse it with chicken broth. Cover with buttered foil or baker's parchment and bake 1 hour.

CORNBREAD
(makes one 9-inch pan, 12 muffins, or a jelly roll pan full for stuffing)

> *1 cup unbleached white flour*
> *1 cup cornmeal*
> *1 tablespoon baking powder*
> *1 teaspoon salt*
> *1 egg*
> *½ cup brown sugar*
> *⅓ cup vegetable oil*
> *1 cup milk*

Preheat oven to 400°F. Prepare pan for baking. (If you wish to bake the cornbread in a cast iron skillet, place a 9-inch cast iron skillet inside the oven while it preheats; otherwise, oil a jelly roll pan or a 12-cup muffin tin.) In a large mixing bowl, combine flour, cornmeal, baking powder, and salt. In a separate bowl, whisk egg with brown sugar and vegetable oil until mixture is smooth, then whisk in milk. Add milk mixture all at once to cornmeal mix-ture and stir just until ingredients are combined. Do not overmix. (If a cast iron skillet is used for baking, remove the hot skillet from the oven and add about 2 tablespoons oil, tilting to coat sides of skillet.) Pour cornbread batter into the prepared pan and bake 10 minutes for muffins, 12 to 15 minutes for a jelly roll pan, or 18 to 20 minutes for a cast iron skillet, or until a knife inserted in the center of the bread comes out clean.

TURKEY LIVER CROSTINI
(makes 12 crostini)

> 3 tablespoons olive oil or butter
> ½ cup finely chopped onion
> 1 teaspoon finely chopped garlic
> 1 turkey liver, finely chopped (this is also
>   good made with chicken liver)
> ½ teaspoon salt, or to taste
> ¼ teaspoon freshly ground black pepper,
>   or to taste
> ¼ teaspoon dried thyme
> ¼ cup Madeira or port
> 12 rounds French bread, toasted

In a sauté pan over medium-high heat, warm olive oil or melt butter. Sauté onion until golden. Add garlic and sauté 1 minute. Add chopped liver, salt, pepper, and thyme and cook 2 minutes, or until liver has lost its color. Pour Madeira or port over mixture and stir until liquid has evaporated. Serve on toasted French bread rounds as an appetizer.

efore I had a pear tree of my own, I used to gather pears from neglected old orchards and even trees behind abandoned houses where I knew the fruit would go unharvested if I didn't intervene. Now I have a pear tree. It came with the house, and in spite of my total neglect the tree in my backyard has produced some beautiful fruit. Unblemished, large and russeted, the pears are more amber than green. They have a good weight in my hand, as if they were carved out of wood, and they make a hollow sound when their skin rubs against my palm. Their smell is not sweet or perfumy; rather it is dry and foresty, like brown leaves. I love them.

Unlike apples or peaches or plums, pears are not best tree ripened but must come off the tree when they are still firm and ripen on their own. Some pear trees will drop their fruit and it will ripen nicely of its own accord wherever it falls, but more often pears seem to need plucking, or they will hang until their texture is ruined. This is the case with the pears in my backyard. Since some of them grow on branches eighteen or twenty feet off the ground, I must climb the tree or use a ladder to gather them.

As soon as one of them tests ready by yielding to a gentle tug, I climb and gather them all. There, under the clear blue sky (for I never gather pears on a cloudy day), I imagine how they will be when they are softer and ripe and when they develop a hint of perfume in their scent. I will slice one on my favorite cutting board, I tell myself as I am reaching as far as I can to pluck it. I have had that particular cutting board for years, and it was hand-made by someone I once knew fairly well. It is too small for chopping vegetables or doing any important work, but it is just the right size for cutting fruit.

Beside the pear, I tell myself, I will place a chunk of cheese, something as soft and perfumy as the pear—fontina perhaps, or maybe a piece of vintage white Tillamook that comes wrapped in black plastic. I once ate a perfectly ripe pear in the south of France with a soft and smelly cheese called Brillat-Savarin after the man who wrote the book on taste. I sipped Muscat de Beaume de Venise that afternoon and listened to sheep announce their reluctance to walk through an area they considered too urban.

If I have enough of the pears, I might preserve some with vanilla beans the same way I can peaches, or I might can them in cheap red table wine with bay leaves and whole black pepper-corns. Certainly I will poach a few that way for dessert on some chilly fall night. Some of the pears will be poached with simple syrup and a vanilla bean, then draped in caramel sauce. Then, if I am feeling particularly ambitious, they will be decorated with caramel shapes to capture the golden light of an autumn after-noon.

Pears, more than any other fruit, have been diversified into a confusion of varieties. Ripening in October and November are hundreds, perhaps thousands, of varieties of pears, of which only a few can be identified with any certainty, and those only by skilled observers. I am not a skilled observer. I regularly encounter pears that I cannot identify. I know only who gave them to me and where they were grown, and I lump them all into one of about five varieties I know.

The pears in my backyard, for instance, defy clear identification. They are something like Bosc. Their skin has that same russeted texture, but their shape is not so graceful. They might be more closely related to a European variety called Conference. Or they might belong to that group of pears with the French word *beurre* attached to their name, for they do have a buttery texture when they are properly ripe. They do not match descriptions of the several dozen varieties I have found in illustrated guides, and the tree is four score years old and more, so I may never know exactly what they are, but that is just fine.

Some of the pear trees gone wild beside the fields that lie behind my house might be Seckel pears. That small, hard variety is said to be very nice for canning, and so are these little specimens. Since pears without distinction can be obtained for next to nothing, a little expense in the flavoring department seems justifiable. A vanilla bean, a pinch of saffron, or a full-flavored red wine can turn indifferent pears into a memorable dessert. Serve poached pears with crisp cookies or a small scoop of ice cream.

PEARS IN CARAMELIZED RED WINE
(serves 6)

> *3 large, firm pears*
> *1 bottle (750 milliliters) inexpensive*
>   *red wine*
> *2 fresh bay leaves, plus additional*
>   *for garnish*

Pinch crushed black peppercorns
1⅓ cups sugar

With a vegetable peeler or a sharp paring knife, peel pears, cut in half, and remove cores. In a kettle over medium-high heat, combine wine, bay leaves, peppercorns, and ⅓ cup of the sugar. When liquid is boiling, add fruit. Reduce heat to medium and cook gently 20 to 30 minutes, or just until fruit yields easily when pierced with a fork. Fruit may be poached and chilled up to 1 day in advance.

In a clean, dry pan over high heat, stir remaining 1 cup sugar until slightly browned and melted. Carefully pour in 1 cup of the poaching liquid. Mixture will boil up and sugar will harden. Stir 2 to 3 minutes, or until sugar has melted again; then pour this caramel sauce over poached fruit. Serve warm or cold for dessert, garnished with fresh bay leaves, if desired.

VANILLA POACHED PEARS
(serves 6)

>*6 large, firm pears (or 12 very small ones)*
>*4 cups water*
>*2 cups sugar*
>*1 vanilla bean*
>*Caramel Sauce (recipe follows)*

With a vegetable peeler, peel pears, but leave stems intact. In a saucepan over medium-high heat, combine water and sugar. With a paring knife, split vanilla bean lengthwise and scrape out seeds. Add vanilla seeds and pod to syrup and bring liquid to a boil. Drop in peeled pears, reduce heat to low, and simmer 25 minutes, or just until fruit yields easily when pierced with a fork. Serve warm or cold with caramel sauce. Poached pears will keep, refrigerated in their syrup, for up to 1 week.

CARAMEL SAUCE
(makes about 1½ cups)

> *1 cup sugar*
> *1 cup whipping cream*
> *⅛ teaspoon salt*
> *1 teaspoon vanilla extract*

In a deep, dry saucepan over medium-high heat, stir sugar until slightly browned and melted. Add cream all at once. Cream will immediately boil up and threaten to spill over, and melted sugar will harden into a mass. Stir and cook 3 to 5 minutes, or until sugar has melted again into the boiling cream. Some lumps may remain; these should be strained out.

Transfer caramel sauce to a clean, dry canning jar or a small pitcher, then stir in salt and vanilla extract. Serve with vanilla poached pears or with ice cream. Caramel sauce keeps, refrigerated, for up to 1 week. If crystals form, sauce can be reheated and stirred until smooth.

CARAMEL DECORATIONS
> *⅓ cup water*
> *1 cup sugar*

Spread baker's parchment or aluminum foil over a baking sheet, grease lightly with a very small amount of vegetable oil or butter, and set aside.

In a saucepan over high heat, bring the water to a boil. Stir in sugar and, as soon as it has dissolved, stop stirring. Cover and cook for 1 minute so that steam will wash down any crystals that may have formed on the sides of the pan. Uncover and watch syrup closely, but do not stir. As soon as syrup turns golden brown, remove from heat. Allow syrup to stand 1 minute, or until it appears to be about as thick as honey when pan is swirled. Dip a fork or a spoon into the syrup and drip swirled or abstract designs onto buttered parchment or aluminum foil. Keep the caramel designs thin, or they will be too tough to bite. Cooled, the caramel becomes very hard and crackly. Stand decorations upright in ice cream or on poached fruit or other desserts. Loosely covered at room temperature, caramel will keep for several days. In humid weather, it becomes cloudy but slightly softer and easier to eat.

winter

A nor'easter's coming," said the clerk at the drugstore when I asked her if there were any more batteries to be had. "The batteries sold out at ten o'clock this morning." This was perhaps the third time that day that I had heard the term "nor'easter," and the phrase was beginning to evoke images of Auntie Em and Uncle Henry saying, "Twister's coming." I wished I had a storm cellar.

That night, freezing winds roared down from the Arctic, across the unprotected plains of western Canada, and down onto the San Juan Islands. Hundred-mile-an-hour gusts punctuated a steady roaring force of air that toppled trees and power lines and froze everything that wasn't safe indoors. The first tree to fall in my yard was an ancient fir that scraped the wall of the house, ripping the power meter off the side on its way down. The next, a particularly large and regal Douglas fir, careened through the lawn furniture and rested its cone-laden tip across the hood of my old green Chevy wagon.

For most of the night, my wife and I kept vigil by candlelight, sipping hot cocoa, turning on the radio now and then to hear how the rest the world felt about our predicament, and wondering where the next tree would fall. I made regular jaunts to the woodpile, climbing over and around the fallen victims of the wind's violent rampage. The fire seemed less and less effective against the cold, and as the evening progressed we closed off rooms and draped blankets over the windows of the rooms we kept open.

My wife made frequent trips to the nursery, where our toddler was sleeping. No trees appeared positioned to fall on his corner of the house, and bundled as he was, he could have survived just about anything. Between these little outings, we huddled close to the woodstove.

With every explosive tree fall, we rushed to the window and rubbed away some of the ice to see where it had landed. The one resting on top of the station wagon was followed shortly afterward by another specimen that missed our Volvo by less than three feet, effectively trapping it in the driveway. Outside, surveying the damage, I stumbled through the branches, then braced myself against the side of the house to look at the sky.

The force of the wind was tangible, like a riptide, and stars blazed in the blackened sky. The house felt small behind my back. I turned to look at it. Bathed in starlight and wreathed in evergreen boughs, its windows glowed with candlelight. It could have been one of those miniature houses set up in department store windows at Christmastime, but it was as though the whole display was inside a wind tunnel.

Back inside, as we nestled in to sleep for a few fitful hours on the couch, we noticed that icicles were forcing their way into the cracks between the metal-framed windows. At a ninety-degree angle to the glass, tiny spears of ice were pointed in at us. I let the blanket fall back over the window and closed my eyes.

The next morning we surveyed the damage. On the single acre we called home, a dozen big fir trees had fallen in the night, crushing at least that many small cedars and madronas on their way down. In the pale gray light of dawn, our indoor campsite looked less charming than it had by candlelight. Getting breakfast was going to be a challenge.

Eighteen-month-old Henry could have raised a fuss when we told him that his toast could not pop up, but in a surprising show of the old stiff upper lip, he happily accepted buttered crackers as a substitute. I stood in the middle of the kitchen, absentmindedly stirring corn syrup into peanut butter, contemplating our next move.

"Are you really going to eat that?" Betsy wanted to know about the peanut butter. Indeed I was. I put water on the camp stove for coffee and spread the stiff, sweetened peanut butter on crackers. Then I shook coffee beans into the electric grinder before I realized that this wasn't going to work. I contemplated smashing the coffee beans with a rolling pin. Then the voice of reason put down her peanut butter cracker and called the next door neighbors to borrow coffee.

With the station wagon pinned under one tree and the Volvo blocked in by another, there wasn't going to be any quick trip to the store. And with the wind still blowing at gale force and the mercury hovering somewhere below ten degrees Fahrenheit, I didn't relish the idea of walking to town. Eventually, though, I mustered my faculties and made my way to the store.

"Yep, it was a real nor'easter," I heard someone say. The word had new meaning now. Hundreds of people seemed to be grocery shopping in the darkened supermarket. A few actually appeared to be Christmas shopping. "The power will stay out until they repair the line from the mainland," explained one of the store's employees to a baffled consumer. "No newspapers, no milk, no bread. The ferries won't be running today in this wind."

"Isn't this terrible?" someone asked, and I realized that she was smiling rather broadly. She looked, in fact, ecstatic. "Oh it's horrible," I agreed, feeling happier than I had in some time. Then I realized that a current of general exhilaration was rippling through the entire crowd. Perhaps everyone was punchy from lack of rest, but this was more than sleep deprivation. It was as if the circus had come to town. This storm was the biggest thing that had happened in ages, and people were loving it.

By dinnertime, the freezing temperatures and the gale force winds had been around for so long that they seemed normal. Every tree that was going to fall seemed already to have fallen. With blankets over the windows and a Coleman stove on the kitchen counter, our home was a post-apocalypse version of the old familiar space we had known and loved in another time.

Still, life must go on, and as the shortest day of the year drew to a close, I set out to make dinner. I heated some olive oil in a soup kettle and tossed in a couple of carrots, cut into matchstick-sized pieces. Next, I salvaged some peas from the freezer, which was by this time roughly the same temperature as the room—too cold for bare fingers and lips but not cold enough for frozen foods to keep.

I sautéed the carrots and peas, added a cut-up breast of chicken, poured in some chicken broth, then seasoned the soup with a slow, dreamy drizzle of some very dark, sweet soy sauce we had found a few years before in Victoria's Chinatown. As an afterthought, I added a hearty splash of Marsala wine. Finally, I broke a bundle of vermicelli noodles over the pot and put a lid on the whole affair. In the darkened house, the simmering pot was very reassuring. The transistor radio offered squeaky Christmas carols as I toasted the last few slices of some homemade bread in a large cast iron skillet.

Made bold by my success with the soup, I made chocolate fudge, and after dinner we played honeymoon bridge, pausing between hands to turn on the radio and hear our predicament cele brated over the airwaves with the same ironic enthusiasm I had noticed in town.

The next day the house became a kind of prison. It was too dark to read, and our fear of burning out the batteries forced us to ration our radio time. The wind had settled down, and the thermometer seemed to be frozen in place.

In our efforts to free the car, we neglected the house, and we discovered around noon that the pipes had frozen. While we had been able to tolerate life without power fairly well, life without water was not an option. I hauled enough water from town to wash and cook and then settled down to stare at the ceiling for a while. I probably would have succumbed to some kind of catatonia in a matter of hours, but Betsy—whose lunacy took a sudden creative bent—pulled out a backpack and started packing a lunch. She made sandwiches with white cheddar cheese and sweet pickle relish; she stuffed pears and oatmeal cookies in the backpack and filled a thermos with hot tea.

"Let's go see Jackle's Lagoon in the ice!" she said, and her suggestion was like a battle cry. We bundled Henry, leaving just enough of his face exposed to ensure that he could breathe, then set out.

The stillness in the woods was like music. And the wind,

exhausted after blowing hard for so long, settled into a pattern of gusts that idly tossed the treetops against a sky as blue as forget-me-nots. We climbed over fallen trees and braved the remains of one of our favorite trails until we came out at the lagoon. There, with the lagoon at our backs, we stood looking out over Griffin Bay, our baby in one backpack and the picnic supplies in another. When we spread our little repast on a fallen tree, our woolly mittens stuck to the sandwiches and the tea froze in the cups. But we were in the light and air, and we were happy.

Now winter picnics are something of a tradition in our family. Cold is made more endurable by walks, and walks in the cold are made infinitely more appealing by the promise of something good to eat along the trail. Sandwiches are all right for these occasions, but something more substantial is better. First, a strenuous walk up a hill to a place with a wide open vista, preferably out of the wind, then fried chicken, apples, hot tea, and delicately spiced oatmeal cookies; these are the things that picnic dreams are made of, any time of year.

SPICY FRIED BREASTS OF CHICKEN
(serves 4)

1 cup buttermilk
1 teaspoon hot pepper sauce
4 boneless, skinless chicken breast halves
1 cup flour
1 teaspoon baking powder
1 teaspoon salt
1 teaspoon paprika
½ teaspoon ground black pepper

½ teaspoon dried thyme
¼ teaspoon ground nutmeg
Vegetable oil for frying

In a nonreactive glass or ceramic bowl, combine buttermilk and hot pepper sauce and immerse chicken breasts in this mixture. Cover and marinate several hours or overnight.

In a self-sealing food storage bag, combine flour, baking powder, salt, paprika, pepper, thyme, and nutmeg. Drop marinated chicken breasts one at a time into flour mixture and shake to coat.

In a large frying pan with a close-fitting lid, pour enough vegetable oil to form a layer ½ inch deep. Heat oil until it registers 375°F on a thermometer, or until a cube of bread floats immediately to the top, bubbles, and turns golden brown in 1 minute. Arrange breasts in a single layer in the frying pan. Reduce heat to medium, cover, and fry 8 minutes. Uncover, turn chicken, and fry 5 minutes more, or until nicely browned. Drain on a brown paper bag. Serve hot or cold.

189

OATMEAL COOKIES WITH DRIED TART CHERRIES AND CRYSTALLIZED GINGER
(makes 3 dozen large cookies)

1 cup unsalted butter, melted
2 cups brown sugar, packed
2 eggs
1 teaspoon vanilla extract
1½ cups unbleached flour
1 teaspoon baking powder
1 teaspoon salt
3 cups quick-cooking oatmeal

1 cup dried tart cherries
½ cup sliced almonds
¼ cup crystallized ginger, chopped

Preheat oven to 325°F. Line jelly roll pans or cookie sheets with baker's parchment. In a large mixing bowl, whisk together melted butter and brown sugar. Stir in eggs, one at a time, beating well after each addition, then stir in vanilla and set aside.

In a separate bowl, whisk together flour, baking powder, and salt. Add flour mixture, oatmeal, dried cherries, sliced almonds, and ginger all at once to butter mixture, then stir just until mixture comes together to form a dough.

Turn dough out onto a floured surface and, with a dough cutter or a knife, divide into thirds. Cut each third into a dozen pieces. (Pieces need not be any particular shape, but cutting dough is swifter than spooning it.) Arrange pieces 2 inches apart on parchment-lined baking sheets and bake 18 to 20 minutes, or until golden brown.

The word "stew" used to mean something different than it does today. When it first slipped into the English language as *stuwen* during the 1300s, it echoed the French word *estuve,* which meant steam bath. French nobility had lifted the Latin word *extupe* or *extufare,* which meant hot air bath. (By another route, the same Roman word for hot air bath eventually became our modern word "stove.")

So stew and stove are close cousins, but long before it came to rest on the stove, "stew" spun off on a tangent and came to mean a brothel, because the places where steam baths were offered were the same places where certain other services were performed. (Streets in England known for their brothels are still referred to as "the stews.")

This other use of the word would not have been missed by cooks who worked in medieval kitchens, where the modern meaning of the word came into full flower. Undoubtedly the bawdiness of the term made it more fun to use and therefore more prevalent. (Professional cooks have always taken some pride in their mastery of the off-color double entendre.)

Before it came to be firmly established in its modern culinary sense, "stew" developed a second identity as a verb, indicating a kind of psychological sweat. A person who stews is one who worries. And before anyone made a dish and called it a stew, it was possible to stew in one's own juices.

Whatever other meanings it may have carried, "stew" now refers first and foremost to a dish cooked by stewing, especially one of meat and vegetables. In America, a stew almost always means a beef stew with potatoes and carrots, a winter dish hearty enough to sustain the fires of life even on the coldest day or night. Surrounding the meat and root vegetables should be a deep brown bath of gravy, brightened here and there perhaps with tomato, green peas, or a bit of chopped fresh parsley. This kind of stew has made such an impression that all other meanings of the word are easily forgotten.

In most formulas for stew, meat is tossed in flour and then browned in oil. On the Gulf Coast, where I grew up, dishes of any consequence, and especially stews, were built upon a slow-cooked mahogany-colored roux of fat and flour. This deep brown base had to be established before any real food entered the stew pot. Into the lava-like pool of browned fat and flour, chunks of beef were stirred. Root vegetables followed the meat: carrots and potatoes, but no turnips or onions. (Onions and garlic were introduced surreptitiously in the form of dehydrated powder.) Finally, a mixture of beef bouillon and coffee was poured over the mixture before it was covered and allowed to simmer for an hour or two.

As an adult, I have encountered some very interesting stews. I enjoy a good seafood stew with a full complement of fish and crustaceans swimming in a spicy, tomatoey broth. I've had fanciful modern versions of Old World working people's stews, like garbanzo beans in a medley of onions, peppers, and tomatoes. I love Indian vindaloo and I find lamb stew irresistible. Still, to me

beef stew with carrots and potatoes in a rich brown gravy constitutes the quintessential stew.

I enjoy a stew like this most, not in the dining room, or com-
fortably nestled into my own safe kitchen, but when I am outdoors, camping, or pretending to camp, under the stars. I owe this
quirky preference to my childhood.

When my mother, in one of her frequent flights of fancy, determined that her stew could be properly enjoyed only if we ate it
at the beach, the whole family humored her and we began a tradition of transporting supper to the beach whenever it was stew
night. She was forever devising ways to keep life interesting.

The first stew nights on the beach were cool Florida winter
nights, but when stew became an excuse to spend an evening at
the beach, we started asking for it all year long. The stew was fully
prepared at home, then the pot was covered, wrapped in towels,
and held in the car until a fire pit could be dug in the sand. A
charcoal fire was made to blaze in the pit, and when it settled into
a pile of glowing embers, a rack was perched above the fire, and
the stew reheated and simmered while we swam.

Settled into folding chairs on the beach, my parents sipped
chilled pink wine near the fire. While their stew simmered and
their suntanned children drank soda pop from cans and built cas-
tles in the sand, they talked. The roar of the waves and the cry of
the gulls soothed away their cares.

When it was determined that the stew was ready, or when all
life's problems had been solved, we sat on our towels in a circle
around the fire. The beef and vegetables were eaten with white
bread and butter on paper plates nestled into those funny rattan
plate holders that were still new back then. The stew pot was bot-
tomless. We all had seconds, and in the fading light our faces

caught the glow of the fire and turned various shades of gold and rose. If there was ever any dessert on those days when we had supper on the beach, I have forgotten it. Perhaps we toasted marshmallows or ate store-bought cookies from the bag.

After dinner, when the stars came out, we lay on our backs and looked for satellites. It seemed to me that there were always astronauts in orbit in those days, and I wanted to know if one of the passing lights could be one of their space capsules. "Would we be able to see it?" I asked my father, and he said yes, but it would look just like any other satellite.

I think those times when we six children lay quietly looking up at the stars must have made my parents happy. Watching us, with our bellies full of nourishing food and our wondering minds full of happy thoughts, they must have felt that whatever kind of stew they were in, all was well with the world. And indeed it was.

One of these days, I will reinstate the old family tradition and take a stew to the beach. My own beef stew is something like my mother's, but I have never had the nerve or the inclination to put coffee in the stew pot. This is not because it isn't good; it is, but I am partial to a tenderizing splash of red wine.

I also put real onion and garlic in my stew, even though my boys would be happier if I would leave them out and revert to my mother's old trick of sneaking in onion powder. Another difference: I make my roux in a most untraditional way with olive oil instead of shortening or bacon grease. It browns very quickly and must be watched and stirred religiously until it is evenly browned. After the beef goes in, the risk of burning the roux is eliminated, and the cook can relax. Serve beef stew with bread and butter and a simple green salad.

BEEF STEW
(serves 6)

> ½ cup olive oil
> ½ cup flour
> 2 pounds beef stew meat, cut into
>   1-inch cubes
> 1 small onion, peeled and finely chopped
> 4 cloves garlic, peeled
> Generous pinch dried thyme
> Few grinds black pepper
> 1 can (22 ounces) tomatoes
> 1 can (17 ounces) beef broth, or 2 cups
>   homemade
> 1 cup red wine or brewed coffee
> 3 medium carrots, peeled and sliced
>   ⅛ inch thick
> 4 large thin-skinned potatoes, such as
>   WhiteRose or Yukon Gold, cut into
>   ½-inch cubes
> 1 package (10 ounces) frozen peas
> Salt to taste

In a large stew pot with a heavy base, cook oil and flour over medium-high heat, stirring constantly, for 6 to 8 minutes, or until flour is nicely browned. (If left unstirred for even a moment, the flour may burn; if it does, discard the roux and begin again.) When you have a smooth, evenly browned base with no black specks, stir in beef. Add onion, garlic, thyme, pepper, tomatoes, beef broth, and wine or coffee. Bring the liquid to a boil, reduce heat to medium-low, and cook 1 hour, stirring from time to time to prevent sticking.

Add carrots, potatoes, and peas and cook 30 minutes longer, or until potatoes are tender. Taste and add salt as desired. At this point, stew may be transported to the beach to be reheated over a charcoal fire or simply allowed to simmer a few minutes longer while the table is set. Serve hot with fresh bread and butter and a simple green salad.

Throughout the ages, any number of foods have been associated with improving the quality of the union of men and women. Tiny threads of saffron and even pinches of powdered rhinoceros horn have been slipped like potions into otherwise innocent formulas for sauce or stew with the secret intent of winning the affection of another. But of all the foods ever attributed with the power of increasing human ardor, none has been so vehemently endorsed as the oyster.

"There are many reasons why an oyster is supposed to have this desirable quality," wrote the late M.F.K. Fisher. "All of them are fond but false hopes." But Mrs. Fisher herself did as much as anyone to romanticize the shellfish in her 1941 classic *Consider the Oyster*.

I read *Consider the Oyster* in early 1990, when Henry was a baby and Betsy and I were idling away a few weeks off from work. I wrote to Mrs. Fisher in care of her publisher and told her that I liked the book and would like to meet her. She replied at once and invited us to come as quickly as possible to Sonoma County, where she lived. She included her phone number so that we wouldn't have to waste time with the mail. I called, and we settled on a trip that would commence immediately. A follow-up note gave detailed directions to her home.

When I realized that I would be cooking a Valentine's Day supper for the first lady of American food letters, I knew that the menu would have to begin with oysters.

Betsy and I selected the oysters ourselves—three dozen perfect Westcott Bays from San Juan Island—and carried them in an ice chest in the trunk of our car to Fisher's Last House, as she called it, in Glenn Ellen, California. The cooler also held racks of Ellensburg lamb, a jar of homemade lavender jelly, sweet Washington pears, and cheese made by Benedictine nuns on Shaw Island, but these other gifts might as well have stayed at home. She only had eyes for the oysters.

Before I unpacked them, I asked, "How's your appetite?" and she answered, "Not much." But when the oysters appeared there was a distinctive elevation of her already high and carefully appointed eyebrows. Her face brightened. Indeed her whole body seemed to respond as she sat a little taller in her wheelchair and offered advice on how to cope with the imagined inadequacies of her kitchen.

"I used to know where everything was," she managed to say, her voice weak with the ravages of a disease that was soon to take her life. "Now I don't know what goes on in there. If you can't find something, just open all the cabinets and throw everything on the floor."

At her neighborhood store, I had purchased organically grown lemons, limes, and oranges. I took off curls of their colorful outer rind with a zester and combined the colorful, fragrant strands with sections of the citrus pulp, crushed coriander seeds, and pinches of sugar, salt, and pepper. I piled crushed ice onto

Fisher's gypsy-green plates, chipped in the course of several transatlantic journeys from Provence. Each shucked oyster received a generous spoonful of the citrus salsa and rested nobly in the ice, but not for long.

In an instant, the oysters had passed Mrs. Fisher's lips, painted a glamorous red for the dinner hour, and the shells lay willy-nilly, exhausted on their bed of ice. Then her ancient voice recovered one of its girlish tones and she asked coyly if her helper, somewhat squeamish about oysters, intended to finish hers. She had barely tasted one and was shyly trying to balance a section of orange on her fork.

"No," admitted the girl. "I don't really know how to eat oysters. Would you like to finish mine?"

"I really would," said Fisher, and a second plate of oysters disappeared. Then she told us stories of her life in France. How, as a younger woman, she had met Colette and suspected her of envy. Colette had taken the young American's hands and said the only way to tell a quality person was by the shape of her fingers. Fisher's hands, according to Colette, were nothing special. Now the hands, frozen by arthritis and Parkinson's disease, were held for us to see over the empty oyster shells, living proof that they had been something special after all.

The roasted rack of lamb with sautéed greens and potatoes, slowly browned in olive oil and rosemary, did, as I had hoped it would, remind Mrs. Fisher of her beloved Provence. "I'm so glad you put lavender instead of mint with the lamb," she said, but she didn't care to eat it. "I'll try it tomorrow for lunch. I don't want to lose the flavor of those oysters."

"People say oysters are supposed to increase one's capacity for

199

physical love," she mused. "But that isn't really it at all, you know." She managed a sip of her wine, both hands on the glass, and we wondered what she would say next.

"No," she went on, carefully replacing the glass on the table. She ran a stiff finger along the edge of one of the gypsy-green plates. "It's just that they're so marvelously light, they don't dull a person's senses." Her voice was failing and it was difficult for her to speak, but we understood what she meant. Oysters instead of a large meal were better than oysters in addition to a large meal.

Then she announced that she had been sitting up too long and wished to lie down. Her helper rose to wheel her across the entry hall, with its Chinese red walls and a little Matisse in a gold frame, into the house's only other room, her bedroom. "You may come and read to me, though," she said as she was wheeled away. "I'd like to hear what you've written about oysters."

So I read to her about oysters, then about citrus fruits and chocolate; I read for hours, and with one hand thrown over her face she listened. "Oh, I can't bear it anymore!" she claimed at one point, then in the same breath, "Read that one again." And so I did, then she said, "That sounds awful! I remember the way we used to cook green beans with bacon until they were all gray mush. Read me another one!"

She was young again and laughed through her old body about bad salad dressings and bad people. She read between the lines that I was raised a Catholic. "But you're a Protestant now, of course," and so we talked about our faith. "The only good thing ever written," she stated in characteristic exaggeration, "was the King James Bible."

"I wish someone would write about putting out all the right

ingredients before getting started," she said at one point. "I don't like the way everyone makes substitutions for everything. *Mise en place,* the French call it. Write about that." Then she was tired, and so I left her.

After that night, I sent iced boxes of Westcott Bay oysters to Mary Frances for several Christmases. "Dear Greg, Betsy, and Henry," said one note, "M.F.K. Fisher thanks you very much indeed for the beautiful oysters," It was signed by her secretary. She died before we had another chance to cook her dinner. Fortunately, there are still opportunities to serve oysters to other people, and chilled with three citrus fruits is one way that makes them happy. If I had another opportunity to serve Mary Frances oysters, I might serve them baked with forest mushrooms. However I prepared them, they wouldn't be a first course; they would be the only course. I think she would prefer it that way.

OYSTERS WITH THREE CITRUS FRUITS
(serves 4 as a light appetizer,
or 2 as a first course)

> 1 red grapefruit
> 1 lime
> 1 orange
> 1 teaspoon chopped garlic
> 1 teaspoon sugar, or to taste
> ½ teaspoon ground coriander seed
> ¼ teaspoon each salt and white pepper
> 1 dozen fairly large Westcott Bay or other
>   Pacific oysters

With a special citrus zester (available at kitchen shops) or an ordinary grater if you don't have a grater, remove colorful outer rind (the zest) from each fruit. Place citrus zest in a small bowl. With a very sharp paring knife, cut top and bottom from each zested fruit, then cut away and discard remaining peel and white pith. Holding fruit over the bowl containing the zest, cut out sections of pulp. Align blade with one of the membranes separating the sections of pulp and cut toward the center of the fruit; at the core, turn the knife and guide blade outward along the next membrane. Repeat to remove the pulp from each segment of fruit. When segments are removed, squeeze any juice left in the core into bowl with zest and pulp segments. Gently stir in garlic, sugar, coriander, salt, and pepper. Citrus fruits may be prepared ahead up to this point and kept covered and refrigerated several hours or overnight.

Just before serving, shuck oysters and arrange round side down on a bed of crushed ice; set aside. Spoon seasoned fruit sections over shucked oysters and serve at once.

OYSTERS BAKED WITH FOREST MUSHROOMS
(serves 6 as a first course, or 4 as a light main dish)

2 dozen large oysters
½ cup water
2 egg yolks
½ cup sherry
¼ cup butter
¼ cup flour

*¼ pound shiitake caps or other forest
    mushrooms, finely chopped*
Salt and pepper to taste
½ cup bread crumbs
¼ cup grated Parmesan cheese

In a large, covered kettle over high heat, steam oysters with ½ cup water for 10 minutes, or until some of the oysters have opened. Remove from heat, and when oysters are cool enough to handle, open with an oyster knife. Arrange opened oysters in a single layer on a baking sheet, keeping them upright; set aside. Strain and reserve steaming liquid.

In a small bowl, stir together egg yolks, sherry, and 1 cup oyster steaming liquid; set aside.

In a small saucepan over medium heat, combine butter and flour and cook, stirring, until golden. Add mushrooms and cook, stirring gently, 3 to 5 minutes, or until mushrooms are softened. Pour egg yolk mixture over mushrooms and cook, stirring, until mixture boils and sauce thickens. Add salt and pepper to taste, then spoon sauce over oysters.

Combine bread crumbs and Parmesan cheese, and crumble mixture over sauced oysters. Oysters may be prepared ahead up to this point and kept refrigerated for several hours.

Preheat oven to 400°F. Bake 10 minutes, or until topping is crisped and lightly browned. Serve hot.

Under the cathedral ceiling of a house on San Juan Island, oranges hang from glossy-leafed branches, shockingly bright against the gray skies and fir trees outside. Athena, the woman who grows them, loves the Pacific Northwest, but like many of us whose genes were forged in warmer climates, she occasionally pines for sunny skies where colorful fruits ripen in the warm air.

"I don't care where I live," she says, "I've got to have my citrus trees." In addition to the orange tree, her living room boasts a lemon tree, and she uses its fruit to make an annual batch of avgolemono soup in honor of her Greek heritage. Her lemons are large and sweeter than the ones I buy. "My lemons are better than anything you can buy at the store," she claims.

Athena's lemons are large, slightly sweet, and very round, more like the lemons that grow in backyards in Florida than the lemons that are grown on anonymous ranches and shipped to our supermarkets. I like to imagine that lemons like these will someday be available in grocery stores. Currently, only one kind of lemon, two or three varieties of orange, and a few types of grapefruit make it to the market, but these are just the tips of some botanical icebergs. A couple of centuries ago, when citrus fruits were all the rage in Europe, several dozen varieties were grown.

When the artist Bartolomeo Bimbi painted a study of citrus fruits for his Medici employers in 1720, some eighty-eight different types were on hand for his still life. The fruits were grown in greenhouses and gardens around a particular estate in Tuscany where the painting still hangs, but the citrus trees have disappeared. Also mostly disappeared are the "orangeries" that once graced every royal palace of consequence in Europe. Especially in cold climates where citrus fruits are disinclined to grow, citrus trees were symbolic of wealth and power, and their fruit was synonymous with good living.

The current generation of professional chefs and discriminating consumers that made obscure produce synonymous with good living in our own time might eventually encourage professional growers to plant some of the more obscure varieties of citrus fruit. Already, unfamiliar cultivars like Meyer lemons, Key limes, and red-fleshed blood oranges are appearing on restaurant menus, and it probably won't be long until they make their debut in supermarkets.

Even if rare and extraordinary citrus fruits were never to make it to our local stores, I would still celebrate the arrival of the more familiar varieties. Every winter, I know that no matter how bleak the weather forecast, all is well with the world because winter weather means the citrus fruits are ripening. The only really good oranges, grapefruits, lemons, and limes ripen in winter.

Because they do ripen in winter, citrus fruits, especially oranges, have become associated with Christmastime. For centuries, they have come onto the market just in time for the holidays. A hundred years ago, even fifty years ago, a single orange in a Christmas stocking could be a big deal. What could be more

205

magical than a ripe, sweet orange from some sunny, faraway place in the middle of a cold, dark winter?

For me, a Florida boy, oranges were not a big deal, and the orange at the bottom of my stocking seemed to be there just to fill out the toe. But my first Christmas season away from home made oranges a little more interesting. I was in a snowbound dorm in Vermont, and as I peeled an orange and ate it section by section at my desk, looking out all the while at the snow coming down on the fir trees that looked like Christmas trees outside my window, it dawned on me that the modern world was a pretty amazing place. There I was, in the far North, eating an orange in a warm room while outside I could have frozen to death. I made a little sketch of the orange peel, curled on my desk like the cocoon from which some fantastic insect might have emerged, and promised myself to appreciate oranges ever more.

In Washington, snowy days and really good oranges are equally rare. When I walk into a grocery store and see oranges piled high under the fluorescent lights, I still feel a little of that wonder that I felt as a college student eating oranges at my desk. And when the little satsuma mandarins appear, I feel very glad indeed, for it was here in Washington that I first encountered these delights.

Satsuma mandarins from California recall the Florida tangerines I liked as a child—not as fragrant perhaps, but juicier, easier to peel, and often sweeter. They are also reminiscent of what I suppose are the best oranges of all, clementines from the south of France. Tiny, outrageously perfumy, and sweet, sweet, sweet, clementines were—for six weeks or so—Henry's favorite food in the world. When we spent a winter in the south of France, the little oranges seemed to be everywhere, and every day he ate as many as we would buy, typically half a kilo, roughly a pound. Now Henry and his brother, Erich, who was conceived that winter, eat satsumas with the same enthusiasm when they come into season around the holidays.

I not only eat them, I also candy the peels for baking. I juice them and transform the juice into sorbet. And at least once a year, I boil the juice into a concentrate that I use instead of vinegar to make salad dressing. Spinach dressed in mandarin orange vinaigrette is the perfect first course for a Christmas dinner.

SPINACH SALAD WITH MANDARIN ORANGES AND PECANS
(serves 8)

> ¾ *cup Mandarin Orange Dressing*
> *(recipe follows)*
> *1 cup Candied Mandarin Orange Peel*
> *(recipe follows)*
> *1 pound spinach leaves, washed and*
> *stems removed*
> *1 cup lightly toasted pecans*

Prepare dressing and candied orange peel.

In a large salad bowl, toss spinach leaves with ¾ cup dressing or enough to generously coat. Transfer to salad plates and top with candied orange peel and pecans.

MANDARIN ORANGE DRESSING
(makes about 1⅓ cups)

> *6 large mandarin oranges, peeled and*
> *divided into segments*

¼ cup lemon juice
1 tablespoon sugar
1 teaspoon kosher salt
¼ teaspoon ground black pepper
1 cup vegetable oil

In a blender, combine mandarin orange segments, lemon juice, sugar, salt, and pepper; purée on high speed until smooth. Strain purée into a saucepan and cook over high heat until reduced to about ⅓ cup. Whisk in vegetable oil and serve, warm, with salad greens.

CANDIED MANDARIN ORANGE PEEL
(makes about 1 cup)

2 cups mandarin orange peel, cut into
¼-inch strips
1½ cups water
1½ cups sugar

Line a baking sheet or a tray with baker's parchment or aluminum foil. In a saucepan over medium-high heat, cover orange peel with the water and sugar and bring to a boil. Reduce heat to low, and allow orange peel to simmer until syrup is mostly absorbed or boiled away. Stir to prevent peels from sticking and burning.

When syrup is almost entirely absorbed or evaporated, transfer orange peel to parchment-lined tray and spread into a single layer. Work quickly to prevent peel from hardening into one massive lump. If peel remains sticky, allow it to air-dry, and sprinkle dry candied fruit with superfine or powdered sugar. Keeps for several months stored in an airtight jar.

very winter the seed catalogs make their rounds, and some of us who should know better spend precious hours of our lives reading about plants we will never grow. With a steady eye—fixed perhaps on the description of some plump Asian cabbages suitable for stir-fry—we sit apparently unmoved while inside our heads we are turning the ground, bringing in extra soil, and even cutting down trees to allow a little extra sunlight.

For several years shortly after Henry was born, the flood of catalogs slowed to a trickle because I had stopped ordering. I knew, and the seed companies seemed to know as well, that in spite of my best intentions I wouldn't really plant the things. Betsy and I were too busy rearing our boys to devote much time to raising vegetables and flowers. I knew other young fathers who managed to maintain gardens when their children were babies, but their gardens were like pampered mistresses and their wives hated every tomato that came out of that seducer of their husbands. Even though it made me feel something like a slug, I had to abandon the garden for a few years.

I began to eye people who had vegetable gardens with a certain amount of awe. They seemed more disciplined than I was. They had better skin and a healthy glow in their eyes. I imagined that they had good time management skills and that they were in touch with the earth in a way that I would never be again. I was keenly aware when the catalog season rolled around. For the seed companies, spring begins when winter is in full swing; the catalogs appear at about the same time the pussy willows come out, shortly after the new year begins, and they induce a sense of urgency about spring that demands attention.

It hurt me that I couldn't keep up. One year, when the first catalog came, I still had seeds from the year before. I hadn't even ordered them. They came as a free gift with some lily bulbs I ordered. I never found time to plant the lilies. When I ordered the bulbs, I was planning a vacation to show the children to their grandparents.

It was during a fit of temporary insanity that I imagined I would have a little spare time to prepare the ground. During the final days before the trip, the lily bulbs kept getting moved from the kitchen table to the windowsill to the desk. Eventually they landed back at the kitchen table with a note for the house sitter, begging her to plant them. The bulbs discreetly disappeared. We never discussed them.

But the seeds that came as a free gift with the bulbs lingered for years. Tucked neatly between the refrigerator and the cabinet above, they stayed in their unopened packets. They were a "heritage collection" of heirloom varieties that once grew in profusion around Monticello, the home of Thomas Jefferson. He had slaves, and that, I supposed, explained how he was able to garden. He had help.

My home is no Monticello. I have no help, and I still don't get most of the seed catalogs, but I am almost free of the guilt they used to induce. A good friend who grows things for me some-times loans me her seed catalogs. "Just look at the pictures," she says, "and help me decide which things to grow."

And so I am at it again, staring at the pictures. I imagine knocking out a wall to install one of those greenhouse rooms for starting the seeds. Then I imagine taking down those fir trees, hauling in a truckload of soil, and putting up a fence to stop the deer from coming in and eating the sprouts. As I fondle the pages and imagine the leaves of corn, green and cool, rising up around me, I hear the voices of Henry and Erich rising to a pitch that in-dicates a need for a referee. Betsy is working hard at something and I feel guilty.

When I regain my senses, I throw the catalog away and re-member the seeds from Monticello. Gardening is much more en-joyable when you are actually doing it than when you are dreaming about it. Still, in the depths of winter, what is one to do? I rally the boys around the stove to get them involved in a project that will keep them from fighting.

It may not be time for planting, but in the kitchen there are other uses for seeds. Poppy seeds for rolls, pumpkin seeds for cookies, and sunflower seeds ground in the food processor with sun-dried tomatoes to form a sort of pesto. It is easy to imagine a whole menu built around seeds. Mixed greens with Sweet Onion and Poppy Seed Vinaigrette (page 58) would get things rolling. If it were the right time of year, crimson poppy petals—which taste like a cross between napa cabbage and snow peas—could be strategically woven through the mixed greens. More fanciful of-ferings would follow.

BREASTS OF CHICKEN IN A SESAME SEED CRUST

(serves 4)

4 chicken breast halves, skinned and boned
½ cup flour
2 egg whites
1 teaspoon kosher salt
2 tablespoons water
1 cup sesame seeds
¼ cup vegetable oil
Ginger and Sesame Sauce (recipe follows)

With the side of a knife, pound chicken breast halves against a cutting board to flatten slightly; set aside. Place three wide-open soup plates or deep dinner plates on a countertop. Into the first plate, measure the flour. In the second plate, stir the egg whites briefly with salt and water; do not whip. In the third plate, spread the sesame seeds.

Roll a half-breast of chicken in flour and shake off excess, then dip in egg white, allowing excess to drip back into bowl. Roll flour-and-egg-coated breast half in sesame seeds to coat, and set aside. Repeat this process—flour, then egg white, then sesame seeds—with remaining chicken breasts. Chicken may be prepared ahead up to this point and held, refrigerated, for several hours.

In a large sauté pan or skillet over medium-high heat, heat oil until hot but not smoking. Arrange sesame seed–coated breast halves in pan in a single layer. Reduce heat to medium and cook 6 to 8 minutes, or until breasts are evenly browned on the underside; then turn and cook 5 to 7 minutes longer. Fully cooked, the meat will be resilient when pressed with a fingertip, and when it is poked with the tip of a sharp knife, the juices will run clear. Transfer cooked chicken breasts to a warm platter, pour off any oil left in the pan, and prepare Ginger and Sesame Sauce in the same pan.

GINGER AND SESAME SAUCE
(serves 4)

> *¼ cup soy sauce*
> *¼ cup dry sherry*
> *¼ cup chicken broth or water*
> *1 tablespoon freshly grated gingerroot*
> *1 tablespoon cornstarch*
> *1 tablespoon toasted (dark) sesame oil*

In a small bowl, whisk together soy sauce, sherry, chicken broth or water, ginger, cornstarch, and sesame oil. Pour all at once into hot sauté pan in which sesame chicken has been sautéed. Over high heat, stir with a wire whisk 10 to 15 seconds, or until boiling sauce is translucent and slightly thickened. Pour about 2 tablespoons of sesame sauce onto each serving plate, and place sesame seed–crusted breast half on top.

PUMPKIN SEED SHORTBREAD
(makes 12 large wedges)

> *1 cup green pumpkin seeds, or "pepitas"*
> *1 cup butter, softened*
> *½ cup powdered sugar*
> *½ teaspoon salt*
> *2 cups flour*

Preheat oven to 375°F. Spread pumpkin seeds out on a jelly roll pan and toast 3 minutes; turn and toast 2 minutes more. Cool seeds completely.

In a mixing bowl, combine softened butter, sugar, and salt. Add flour and toasted pumpkin seeds all at once. Stir just until flour is moistened; do not overmix. Dough will be dry. Transfer to a 10-inch pie pan and press flat. Bake 15 to 18 minutes, or until golden brown. Slice, while still hot, into 12 wedges. Cool before serving.

At the great round table where I took most of my meals as a child, real butter seldom appeared. In summer, ubiquitous whipped margarine was melted over corn on the cob, spread on toast, and stirred into batters, but real butter in pale, cold sticks was usually there, stored discreetly in the refrigerator and—like the good china—brought out only on special occasions.

The special occasions that called for good china were always public events—dinner parties and holidays—but the occasions for real butter were private. My mother, on quiet winter mornings alone or when her mother was visiting, would bring out the butter and melt it over hot biscuits or toast, savoring it along with her rare moments of peace and quiet. We kids only saw this sort of thing when we were home sick from school. Perhaps this is why I crave butter more in winter than in summer.

"You wouldn't like this," she said, and for a while we believed her. "Your grandfather," she added, spreading a little of the forbidden yellow fat along a piece of crust, "wouldn't allow margarine in the house. But when real butter was rationed during the war, Grandma had to buy margarine and she hid it from him. It came in white blocks with a little packet of yellow dye that had to be stirred in."

I imagined my grandmother surreptitiously preparing the spread and hiding the evidence. Coming from a dairy family herself, it must have been very strange for her. Perhaps, I thought, she felt it her patriotic duty to perform the clandestine kitchen ritual.

"Your grandfather never noticed."

This part I could not believe. I had tasted on the sly the forbidden butter and knew its wild and distinctive flavor was completely unlike margarine, so bland and familiar that it had no taste at all. Anyone would notice the difference between butter and margarine, I thought, and especially the legendary gastronome who was my grandfather.

Perhaps my grandfather did notice the switch and chose to keep quiet. Who was fooling who?

There's no sense in fooling anyone when it comes to cooking and baking with butter. Butter handles differently than margarine. On the stove it can be stirred into sauces to create smooth emulsions that melt like fine chocolate in the mouth. Margarine collapses when any attempt is made to transform it into sauce, and even if its synthetic structure held, its artificial flavor would ruin the finished sauce. When the whey is cooked out of it, butter can be clarified into a versatile fat that takes on a nutty glow and withstands high temperatures for quick frying. With margarine this is out of the question. In the oven, butter forms delicate, flaky layers in pastry and shortens cakes with incomparable smoothness. Margarine just isn't quite the same.

With about 80 percent fat and 20 percent water and milk solids, dairy butter is unique among kitchen fats and oils. Flavor aside, it is inimitable in other ways. Softer margarine with less saturated fat typically contains more water and is therefore less suitable for frying, and while it can make a decent cake, it is not well suited for pie crusts and other pastries. Shortening and lard, with no water at all, are better butter substitutes for these purposes, but of course they lack the delicate taste of butter.

Personally, I would rather have a sliver of something made with butter than a great pile of something else made with margarine or shortening. I think the substitutes leave us hungry no matter how much we eat because they do not satisfy our innate sense of goodness. Imitations of any kind do not fill our very real need for something good and true.

Of course, health concerns drive some people away from butter and into the clutches of its imitators, but I can't help wondering if they might not be better off eschewing the substitutes and allowing themselves an occasional bit of the real thing. Certainly none of us needs to gorge on large amounts of any fat, least of all one as saturated as butter, so it is wise to find ways of making a little go a long way.

One way to derive more flavor from less butter is to brown it slightly. European cooks have done this for centuries, but they perfunctorily add lemon juice or vinegar to their browned butter to create an impromptu sauce for vegetables, so the phrase "browned butter" has come to denote a tangy sauce made with browned butter and not the stuff itself. In India and parts of the Near East, lightly browned, clarified butter called "ghee" or *samna* is made by boiling out the whey in whole butter. The resulting amber fat is a staple that stays fresh without refrigeration and serves as a foundation for frying and baking.

Whenever I serve something baked or fried with amber butter, someone invariably asks how that incredible flavor was achieved. Many are sure that some special spice previously un-known to them has been discovered in my kitchen. When I tell them that there is no spice, that it's only butter, they think I'm keeping a secret. Keep amber butter around for sautéing greens or crisping vegetables in the oven. Drizzle a little over steamed win-ter squash, use it to make toast in a skillet, or use it in place of whole butter in a favorite recipe for cookies or cake. You will be pleased.

AMBER BUTTER, OR GHEE
(makes about 1¾ cups)

1 pound unsalted butter

In a large saucepan over medium heat, melt butter and sim-mer steadily 10 minutes, or until foam rises. Watch closely to pre-vent boiling over. As it foams, stir it down. When any water that was trapped in the butter has boiled away and the foam on top is beginning to brown, remove from heat and pass hot fat through a fine strainer. Use amber butter, or ghee, in place of whole butter when sautéing. Amber butter keeps at room temperature for sev-eral days or, covered and refrigerated, for several weeks.

KALE SAUTÉED IN AMBER BUTTER
(serves 4)

1 bunch (1 pound) curly green kale
¼ cup Amber Butter (see previous recipe)
Kosher salt and freshly ground pepper

Rinse kale and shake off excess water. Stack leaves with stems pointing in one direction; then, with a sharp knife, trim stems from bunch. Roll trimmed leaves together into a fairly tight bundle and cut across line of stems into ⅛-inch ribbons; set aside.

In a large sauté pan over high heat, melt amber butter and add a generous pinch or two of kosher salt and several grinds of black pepper. Pile in cut kale all at once and, with tongs, lift and turn continually 2 minutes, or until ribbons are wilted and lightly coated in amber butter. Serve at once.

CRISPY POTATOES
(serves 4)

>   ¼ cup Amber Butter, melted (see earlier
>   recipe)
>   2 large baking potatoes, scrubbed
>   Kosher salt

Preheat oven to 350°F. Spread 2 tablespoons of the melted butter onto a jelly roll pan. Hold remaining butter in a warm spot to keep soft. Using a vegetable slicer or a very sharp knife, cut potatoes into paper-thin slices. Spread slices in an even layer on buttered pan, and drizzle with remaining 2 tablespoons butter. Sprinkle with salt and bake 10 minutes, or until golden brown. Free potatoes from pan with a metal spatula; then, with metal tongs, pinch crispy potatoes into bundles to stand more or less up-right on plates. Serve hot.

When I first discovered home preserving, I wanted to preserve everything in sight. That first year, nothing was safe. Apples from neglected trees all over the neighborhood were captured in jars of jelly and sauce. I didn't wait for tomatoes to ripen; instead, I boiled them with spices and onions to make green tomato chutney. Even the notoriously prolific blackberry vines were hard-pressed to produce enough fruit for my insatiable need to make preserves.

That winter, my little laundry room turned pantry was filled with rows of jars. Dilled green beans, pale pie cherries, pickled carrot sticks, and jams and jellies galore made a colorful patchwork of the room's shelf-lined walls. But I wanted more.

When canning season ended, I scarcely noticed. I perused old books and found more ideas for preserving. Faded peaches from the grocery store bargain bin were transformed into more chutney. Flame grapes with vinegar and allspice became a strange little pickle, and cauliflower gleaned from a friend's garden looked like something preserved in formaldehyde but tasted wonderful, I thought. It was clear to everyone but myself that I had gone overboard.

Finally, other projects commanded my attention, and I stopped preserving. Christmas came and I unburdened myself of a great many jars, transferring the problem of how to use these strange pickles and preserves to my friends. Months went by and I still had a generous year's supply of home-canned goods.

When apples and blackberries began to ripen again, I still had jars of applesauce and jam from the year before. Only canned tomatoes, peaches, and raspberry jam were completely used up. Actually, several years went by before I used all the chutney I made that first year of canning, and my pantry has been known to harbor things that could well be considered antiques.

Now I know that the time between canning seasons is a chance to take stock of what's there, what's worth keeping and what's not. Induced perhaps by a case of cabin fever, Betsy and I clean out the pantry every winter. One year, behind cans of chicken broth, pineapple, and tomatoes, a spilled bag of pine nuts, and three opened bags of rice were some jars of preserves that had been with me for a very long time. There were, among other things, a jar of pickled beets and a couple of jars of faded pie cherries.

"Do you realize," asked my wife, "that you have had these preserves longer than I've known you?" It is true that I had packed and moved with some of those jars three or four times, and I don't move often. What I realized was that the preserves were like a diary.

I remembered picking the pie cherries from a big tree in Bellingham, where some friends of mine were renting an old bungalow on the edge of town. I had stood on a rickety ladder looking out over empty fields that are covered with houses now. A horse grazed in the pasture next door, and children played freeze-tag somewhere behind me. I could hear their laughter and their high-pitched voices, shrill and full of the fear and delight of being tagged. I could hear birds there too, and I had to pick and choose among the cherries because some of them had been pecked. There were no cherry trees where I grew up, and this was the first time I had ever picked cherries from a tree.

The day I picked those cherries, I took them to the little student apartment I had then, and I made a Danish cherry flan from a recipe I found in *Larousse Gastronomique.* I covered some of the cherries with a pint of vodka and spiked that jar with a scoop of sugar and a cinnamon stick to make what my friends with the tree called "cherry bounce." The rest of the cherries I canned in pint-sized jars.

"Get rid of them," I said after a moment. "We'll never eat them. Toss them out! " And so we did. Out went the old pie cherries. Out too went jars of umber-colored corn relish and jars of pickled beets from a garden I had tended in the days when I was still a bachelor, more than a decade before. Everything went into the garbage disposal. "Disgusting," I admitted.

"What a relief!" said Betsy.

"Yuck!" said Erich, who had climbed up on his step stool to watch the canned goods go down the drain.

When all the jars were empty and clean and lined up on shelves in the little broom closet we call the rat room, I began to imagine all the ways I could fill them again. When summer comes, we'll go to Yakima for tomatoes. Tomatoes are my best canned food. I bottle them with a splash of balsamic vinegar and a few leaves of basil. They are always gone long before spring.

Jams and jellies are also well received. We like plum jelly, made from Italian prunes just before they ripen, and Concord grape jelly made from grapes that grow on a vine in my in-laws' backyard. Blackberry and raspberry jams disappear more slowly, but we like them too. My favorite jam is apricot. I like to spread it between the layers of a chocolate cake or bake it between layers of sweet cookie dough or brownie batter full of walnuts.

When the pantry was reorganized and the food we saved was neatly tucked away in bags or stowed in clean, dry jars, I felt inspired to cook again. The pasta was full of promise. The rice was no longer a burden, the jars of preserves were no longer frightening relics. Nearly forgotten treasures like a tin of saffron and an unopened can of whole-bean Italian coffee were pulled to the forefront, so that I would remember to use them. Everything looked good enough to eat. Then we started on the refrigerator.

Like the pantry, our refrigerator is typically stuffed. Some of what's in there really shouldn't be. The condiments alone take up most of the space: mayonnaise, three kinds of mustard, ketchup, teriyaki sauce, and three kinds of salsa. By the time everything that needed to be composted was removed and the shelves were wiped down, we were beginning to think about lunch. In the produce drawer there remained one good-looking sweet potato, half an onion, and half a bunch of kale. I determined at once that this would become a kind of stew to be served with rice. Sweet potatoes, cooked on the stovetop, become tender in an incredibly short time, so start the rice before you start the stew.

KALE AND SWEET POTATO STEW
(serves 2)

> *½ large yellow onion*
> *1 large yam or sweet potato*
> *4 or 5 leaves curly green kale*

223

> *2 tablespoons vegetable oil or ghee*
> *½ teaspoon ground ginger*
> *¼ cup water*
> *¼ cup teriyaki sauce*
> *1 cup rice, cooked according to package*
> *   instructions*

Peel onion and slice lengthwise into ⅛-inch slices; set aside. Peel sweet potato and cut it into 2-by-¼-inch matchsticks; set aside. Rinse kale and shake off excess water. Cut across line of stems into ¼-inch ribbons.

In a saucepan over high heat, heat oil and drop in sliced onion, sweet potato, and kale. With tongs, toss vegetables in hot oil 1 minute, or until wilted and just beginning to brown. Sprinkle dried ginger over mixture and toss for a few seconds to coat. Add water and teriyaki sauce all at once, then cover, reduce heat to low, and simmer 10 minutes, or just until sweet potato is tender. Uncover, turn heat to high, and cook 1 minute, or until sauce surrounding vegetables is almost evaporated. Serve hot with rice.

CROSTATA (RUSTIC ITALIAN JAM TART)
(serves 6)

> *2 cups flour*
> *½ cup sugar*
> *¼ teaspoon salt*
> *½ cup cold butter, cut into bits*
> *1 egg*
> *1 egg yolk*
> *2 tablespoons water*
> *1 cup homemade jam or marmalade*

Preheat oven to 350°F, and line a baking sheet with baker's parchment. In a food processor or mixing bowl, combine flour, sugar, and salt. Add butter and pulse motor on and off or work in until mixture is evenly crumbly. Add egg and egg yolk and pulse motor or stir with a wooden spoon to form a smooth dough.

Set aside one-third of the dough. On parchment-lined baking sheet, roll or pat remaining two-thirds of dough into a 10-inch circle. Fold the sides up to form a raised lip around the edges; set aside. Stir water into jam or marmalade and spread jam mixture over rolled dough. Roll reserved dough into several pencil-sized coils and lay these in stripes over jam. Bake 30 minutes, then remove from oven and cool for at least 30 minutes before slicing.

For those of us who live in a climate that is mild and for the most part very gentle, a spell of bad weather, especially very bad weather, can be, in spite of all the discomfort it brings, a happy occasion. It draws us together. In a perverse way, it entertains us. It presents us with challenges that force us to rely on our wits to maintain simple homeostasis. A threat to our survival, at least one as ambivalent as the weather, can be a welcome stimulant.

One year, when a particularly bitter little nor'easter blew in and froze everything that wasn't able to run for cover, my family bundled up and left the house just after dawn to catch a ferry. Ordinarily we drive to the ferry, but this time we didn't drive, we walked. My in-laws were going to meet us on the mainland to deliver their dog to us. While they vacation in Hawaii, their dog, Corky, vacations with us in the San Juan Islands. In the eerie predawn darkness we tilted our bodies headlong into the wind and made our way down deserted streets to the frozen dock, where the ferryboat rocked in the wild winter waves. Erich, riding on my shoulders, cried out that his hands were cold, and Henry ran ahead, shouting, "This is fun!"

We ran on board, sliding on the icy deck, and scurried up the stairs. From our old canvas bag, Betsy pulled a thermos of coffee and a linen towel full of hot biscuits. There in the galley, we ate fresh biscuits with butter and honey. We poured hot coffee into mugs from home, and the boys drank ice water from paper cups. We were happy as larks.

The ferry swayed back and forth, high and low. One moment, all we could see was water; the next, all we could see was sky. The islands we passed were pale, icy versions of their ordinary selves, and the rocks on shore were white with frozen sea foam. Whitecaps rose and fell and splashed against the islands and against the ferry, and we raised our eyebrows at the boys until they laughed out loud, and we laughed too because the rocking boat made us foolish and because we were glad to be alive.

When at last we reached the mainland, we disembarked from the car deck. As we walked off in front of the cars, tugging our scarves, our children staying close, we laughed again because it was a challenge to walk against the ferocious wind, even that short distance to the ferry terminal. But Erich clung to his mother and Henry clung to me, and we could have been in a foreign country, or just coming to America for the first time; everything seemed so new and unfamiliar in its twinkling coat of ice. Even the air sparkled with ice crystals no larger than specks of dust.

In Anacortes, we met Betsy's parents and they delivered Corky. It was a silly reason to travel so far in such cold weather, but all of us were glad and everyone patted the little dog, and someone said, "See what we go through for you!" Corky wagged his tail and panted as if to show that he knew very well, and he was as happy and cold as the rest of us were.

Before we caught the next ferry home, my in-laws treated us all to a late breakfast at a restaurant in Anacortes, and my boys told their grandparents everything they had to tell, and my in-laws told us all they had to tell. When all the talking was done, Henry drifted over to the pastry case and fell in love with a chocolate cream pie.

"It's perfect," he said. "See how the cream filling looks so smooth, and the whipped cream is piled up so high? I could eat the whole thing!" I explained that we don't have dessert after breakfast, and he begged to differ. I squatted to his level and saw that it was indeed a magnificent pie. It had a graham cracker crust and the smoothest-looking filling I had ever seen. The whipped cream on top of the chocolate cream seemed, from his perspective, to mound up as high as a snow-covered mountain. Just when I was on the brink of joining forces with him and buying a slice of pie, it occurred to me that I would have as much fun making a pie like that as he would have eating it, and so I promised that when we got home we would make a pie of our own.

The ferry ride home was a subdued replay of the ride to the mainland. Corky whined hysterically at the idea of having to ride on the car deck and earned himself an invitation to ride in someone's car. We gazed quietly out the windows on the way home, lulled by the rocking ferry, our bellies full of brunch.

At home, Betsy put Erich down for a nap and put herself into a deep, sweet-smelling bubble bath. Henry and I spent the rest of the afternoon in the kitchen making pie. We crushed graham crackers for the crust. We melted chocolate into silky custard for the filling and whipped a pint of cream for the topping. That night, we all had pie for dessert, and it was too rich. We had it again the next night, and it seemed even richer, and there was pie for after-school snacks the day after that.

I will never see a chocolate cream pie again without also seeing, in my mind's eye, the faces of Henry and Erich and the icy waves. I will feel the salty wind in our faces and remember Betsy's laughter and Corky's antics and the sheer delight we all feel when a day is completely different from other days.

WINDY DAY CHOCOLATE CREAM PIE
(makes one 10-inch pie, to serve 8 to 12)

2 cups graham cracker crumbs
½ cup brown sugar
½ teaspoon ground cinnamon
½ cup butter, melted
Chocolate Cream Filling (recipe follows)
2 cups whipping cream
½ cup powdered sugar
1 teaspoon vanilla extract

In a food processor or large mixing bowl, combine graham cracker crumbs, brown sugar, cinnamon, and melted butter. Press the crumbly mixture into the sides and bottom of a 10-inch pie plate and chill. Prepare chocolate cream filling, transfer into crumb crust with a rubber spatula, and refrigerate until completely cooled. Whip cream; stir in powdered sugar and vanilla. Pile whipped cream into a large, self-sealing food storage bag and snip off 1 inch from the corner. Squeeze whipped cream from the open corner onto chilled pie filling. Serve cold. Pie keeps, covered and refrigerated, for 2 days.

CHOCOLATE CREAM FILLING
(makes about 3 cups, to fill one 10-inch pie)

> *⅔ cup sugar*
> *½ cup flour*
> *½ teaspoon salt*
> *2 eggs*
> *2 cups milk*
> *1 cup semisweet chocolate chips*

In a medium saucepan, combine sugar, flour, and salt. With a wire whisk, beat in eggs; when mixture is well combined, stir in milk. Cook over medium-high heat, stirring constantly, until custard just begins to boil. Continue to cook, stirring, 1 minute, then remove from heat. Stir chocolate chips into hot custard. Transfer custard to crumb crust–lined pie pan and chill.

he line between winter and spring, or between any two seasons, is often a hazy one. Sometimes the first day of spring is colder than the last day of winter, the first day of fall hotter than the last day of summer. Solstices and equinoxes are arbitrary ways to mark seasons that seem capricious and blurred around the edges. Wasn't it spring when the first forsythia bud impatiently opened in February? Or when the light pouring into the kitchen was suddenly so warm and bright that we had to stop what we were doing to stand and consider for a moment that we were living on a spinning orb?

Property boundaries on San Juan Island are sometimes as wonderfully blurry as the borders between the seasons, and on our walks around the island, we sometimes slip from national park or county park onto private property and then back onto public land without encountering any markers or fences along the way. Many of our walks follow trails that are older than any boundaries.

We often walk along the south side of the island, near American Camp, where soldiers during the Civil War era stationed themselves to prevent a British claim on the island from taking hold. Just as often, we walk around a point on the northern end of the island called British Camp, where the British soldiers staked their claim at the same time.

One day, when winter was rapidly dissolving into spring, Betsy and I tried to take a winter walk with the boys along a trail near British Camp. That trail always floods in spring, and every spring we muddy our shoes and say, "Why did we come this way?"

Plum blossoms threatened to open above our heads, and young green grass rose from the mud beneath our feet. Flowering currant blossoms hung, already past their prime, and early daffodils in an abandoned yard opened as if they were still surrounded by a proper garden, tended by invisible hands.

Ki no Tsurayuki, the Japanese poet, once wrote:

> *I went out in the Spring*
> *To gather young herbs.*
> *So many petals were falling,*
> *Drifting in confused flight,*
> *That I lost my way.*

Our feet grew muddier with every step. Henry and Erich had to be lifted up, and we both knew that we should turn back, but we forged ahead. Blackberry vines threatened to block our way, and we could not go off to one side or the other because the mud was too deep. Then we came out into the open fields of British Camp and the Canadian geese honked their disapproval and scattered toward the bay.

Out in the open, the breeze was as cool as the light was warm, and we ran, playing keep-away, first around and through a little garden maze maintained by volunteers from the historical society, then up a high hill to a place where generals' cottages once stood, looking down over the camp. Then we stood breathless at the top of the hill, and Henry ran ahead while Erich lagged behind and we wondered if they would ever simply keep pace.

It grows difficult to remember if it was last year or the year before when we came late and the pear blossoms were already out, or which year it was that we came too early and frost still held the mud in place. "Remember," said little Erich, "when the leaves were here and we rustled and tussled in those big piles?" I remember the dry, crackly leaves, and I smile because to him that was long ago. And indeed, in spring, the fall is long ago and barely real anymore.

What is real, finally, is the way times and places become a part of us, the way the spring light goes right through our flesh and into our hearts and melts our winter-weary thoughts. Light is a soothing balm, as vital and nourishing as a bowl of soup or a loaf of bread, and I like to imagine that some of the light that shines on San Juan Island is woven into my children's lives to nourish them forever.

INDEX